THE CORNING MUSEUM OF GLASS

A Decade of Glass Collecting
1990–1999

Stained glass and wood screen with four panels depicting herons and other birds, panels enclosed in painted and stenciled frames of ebonized wood. England, perhaps designed by John Moyr Smith, about 1875–1880. H. 208.3 cm (94.2.12).

THE CORNING MUSEUM OF GLASS

A Decade of Glass Collecting
1990–1999

by David Whitehouse

The Corning Museum of Glass
Corning, New York

Distributed by Harry N. Abrams, Inc., New York

Editor: Richard W. Price
Photographer (unless otherwise stated):
    Nicholas L. Williams
Designer: Jacolyn S. Saunders

Copyright © 2000
The Corning Museum of Glass
Corning, New York 14830-2253

Distributed by Harry N. Abrams, Incorporated, New York

ISBN 0-8109-6710-3
Library of Congress Catalog Card Number 99-85943

Prepress work coordinated by Graphic Solutions, Corning, New York
Printed in the U.S. by Upstate Litho, Rochester, New York

Harry N. Abrams, Inc.
100 Fifth Avenue
New York, N.Y. 10011
www.abramsbooks.com

CONTENTS

INTRODUCTION:
A Museum Diary

Twenty years ago, Robert J. Charleston published *Masterpieces of Glass*, a selective history of glass and glassmaking based on 100 carefully chosen objects in The Corning Museum of Glass. In 1990, Charleston published an expanded edition of his book, taking the opportunity to include a number of objects acquired in the 1980s. *A Decade of Glass Collecting* brings the roster of many of the Museum's most significant acquisitions up to date.[1]

The Corning Museum of Glass, a nonprofit educational institution, was conceived by Arthur A. Houghton Jr. and the Hon. Amory Houghton as part of the Corning Glass Center, a unique complex that originally consisted of the Museum, a Hall of Science and Industry, and the Steuben Glass factory. The Center was founded by the board of directors of Corning Glass Works (now Corning Incorporated) to mark the 100th anniversary of the company. The Museum, which is dedicated to the history, art, and manufacture of glass, opened in May 1951 with a collection of just over 2,000 objects and a library committed to acquiring everything printed on the history of glass. Today, almost 50 years later, the number of objects in the glass collection exceeds 35,000 and the Rakow Library contains some 70,000 volumes, together with abundant archival and audiovisual materials.

As the glass collection and library grew, so did the scope of the Museum and its facilities. The first volume of the Museum's annual *Journal of Glass Studies* appeared in 1959, providing a vehicle for disseminating the results of research worldwide. The

Five enameled beakers. Four decorated in the studio of Anton Kothgasser, Vienna, about 1820–1828. One (SECOND FROM LEFT) decorated by Gottlob Samuel Mohn (signed), Vienna, about 1811–1820. H. (tallest) 11.0 cm (92.3.15–19). Gift of Mrs. K. F. Landegger.

first *New Glass Review*, a competition intended to identify (then publish) the best of recent art and design, took place in 1977.

Three years later, the Museum moved out of its original home in the Glass Center and took possession of a new, adjacent building designed by Gunnar Birkerts. Birkerts's building sent a message about its contents. Textured glass panels lined with stainless steel sheathe the upper floor, creating a subtle mirrored effect and reflecting solar heat. Below this, a system of real mirrors admits daylight but excludes direct sunlight, which can damage certain types of glass.

In 1996, we created The Studio, which teaches artists and students at all levels of expertise the various processes of glassworking. At the same time, we embarked on a program of renovation and expansion to accommodate new programs and an anticipated increase in the number of visitors. Once more, the new buildings reflect their purpose. The new lobby, designed by the New York firm of Smith-Miller + Hawkinson, is a steel skeleton with a glass skin. The new library, designed by Bohlin, Cywinski, Jackson, announces the nature of its holdings by way of a glass facade. In all of these activities, the generosity and encouragement of Corning Incorporated have been decisive factors in our success.

With the exception of contemporary works of art acquired from the artists or their representatives, and of study material from archeological excavations in countries that allow foreign missions to retain some of the finds, most of our acquisitions come directly or indirectly from private collections.[2] Indeed, the most obvious trend in the history of collecting in the last 100 years or more is the inexorable transfer of art and artifacts from private to public collections. Some of these private collections consist of family heirlooms handed down from one generation to the next, while others (perhaps the majority these days) were formed by individuals.

Although most of our acquisitions (contemporary art excepted) come from private collectors, the character of our collection differs profoundly from that of a private collection. Private collectors, of

Replicas of the Portland Vase. LEFT TO RIGHT: glass version engraved by Franz Paul Zach, about 1862; "first edition" jasperware copy made by Josiah Wedgwood, about 1789–1790; jasperware copy made by Josiah Wedgwood and Sons Ltd. and polished by John Northwood, about 1877–1880; glass blank made by Hodgetts, Richardson and Co., 1878; and glass replica carved by Joseph Locke, 1878. H. (tallest) 28.0 cm (92.3.79, 92.7.2, 92.7.3, 92.2.16, 92.2.15). Clara S. Peck Endowment.

Handkerchief vase, blown and applied. Roman Empire, probably
Syro-Palestinian region, fourth century A.D. H. 7.0 cm (97.1.16).

course (within the constraints of the law and their checkbooks), can collect anything. They have no obligation to define or follow a collecting policy; they are free to pursue personal preferences and to indulge quirks of taste. I have no problem with this. My personal library contains some of the books I want to have at hand, and it is not intended to be an encyclopedic public or college library.

Curators at museums, however, have a different agenda. Within the boundaries set by their charters or mission statements, they have a duty to build collections that are encyclopedic and include examples of work from every pertinent artist, historical period, or region. Successful curators subordinate their personal preferences to the business of collecting things that reflect every facet of their area of responsibility —and reflect it intelligently.

Many assume that, at Corning, we pursue this goal with a colossal budget. This is not the case. The allocation for purchases from the annual operating fund is adequate but not enormous (less than two percent of the total in 2000). We also have income from endowments, and we are fortunate to receive munificent support from donors. Indeed, the history of the Museum is punctuated by gifts. The collection began in 1950 with a gift for the purchase of 213 objects from Steuben Glass Inc., including a Verzelini goblet, a sealed Ravenscroft *roemer*, and a pair of goblets gilded and enameled for the 10th earl of Pembroke

by William and Mary Beilby. Subsequently, Edwin J. Beinecke donated his collection of 16th–18th-century central European enameled glasses in 1957; the Hon. Amory Houghton presented the Museum with his superb collection of paperweights in 1978; the incomparable collection of some 2,400 drinking vessels formed by Jerome Strauss came to us as the bequest of Mr. Strauss and the gift of The Ruth Bryan Strauss Memorial Foundation in 1979; and between 1989 and 1992 Mrs. Juliette K. Rakow gave and bequeathed to the Museum many outstanding pieces from the Rakow Collection of English 19th-century cameo glass. Collectively, these and innumerable other gifts, both great and small, have helped us to build a glass collection that is unsurpassed anywhere in the world.

This book contains images of more than 200 objects representing more than 2,000 years of glassmaking, from the second or first century B.C. to the present.[3] These objects are arranged by curatorial area, and each section is preceded by a brief introduction.

For 50 years, with an extraordinary amount of help from friends all over the world, the Museum has been assembling a collection that celebrates the art and history of glass. We embark on our second half-century with an expanded mission: while continuing to strengthen the existing collection, we are committed to collecting and displaying materials that illustrate the science and technology of glass, and their impact on our daily lives.

To this end, in 1999 we opened the Glass Innovation Center. It is packed with artifacts, images, and interactive devices, arranged in three galleries devoted to vessels, optics, and windows. The Innovation Center has something for everyone, from the preteen brought up on fast-paced, visual information to the scientist or engineer challenging the details of an exhibit. Once again, support from Corning and around the world has played a vital role in filling the galleries with artifacts. Exhibits were lent or donated by NASA, the Smithsonian Institution, the Department of the Navy, and Corning Incorporated, which gave us the "200-Inch Disk": the first, unsuccessful attempt (in 1934) to cast the mirror for the giant telescope at the Palomar Observatory in California.

Who knows? In 2010, perhaps, we shall find ourselves describing a decade of enriching two collections, one dedicated to the art and history of glass and the other dedicated to its science and technology.

David Whitehouse
Executive Director
The Corning Museum of Glass

□
1. Robert J. Charleston, *Masterpieces of Glass: A World History from The Corning Museum of Glass*, New York: Harry N. Abrams Inc., 1980; *idem*, with contributions by David B. Whitehouse and Susanne K. Frantz, *Masterpieces of Glass: A World History from The Corning Museum of Glass*, expanded ed., New York: Harry N. Abrams Inc., Publishers, 1990. The title of the present volume echoes the title of an exhibition of glass from the Melvin Billups Collection, which was shown at Corning in 1962.

2. For example, the Museum holds study collections of fragments of glass from excavations at Jalame, Israel, and Fustat, Egypt. The fragments from Jalame were excavated by a joint expedition of the University of Missouri and The Corning Museum of Glass, and they were released by the Department of Antiquities and Museums of the Government of Israel (Gladys D. Weinberg, ed., *Excavations at Jalame, Site of a Glass Factory in Late Roman Palestine*, Columbia, Missouri: University of Missouri Press, 1988, pp. vii–viii). The material from Fustat was excavated by a team from the American Research Center in Egypt, and it was released by the Egyptian Department of Antiquities (R. H. Pinder-Wilson and George T. Scanlon, "Glass Finds from Fustat: 1964–71," *Journal of Glass Studies*, v. 15, 1973, pp. 12–30).

3. For a brief introduction to the history of glassmaking, see Chloe Zerwick, *A Short History of Glass*, 2nd ed., New York: Harry N. Abrams Inc., Publishers, in association with The Corning Museum of Glass, 1990; and my essay "Glass," in *The Corning Museum of Glass and the Finger Lakes Region*, Corning, New York: The Corning Museum of Glass, 1993, pp. 2–7.

Flask, blown and enameled, inscribed "MAT.ew STUBS Esq./1757." England, possibly Birmingham, dated 1757. H. 16.2 cm (97.2.1).

Ancient and Islamic Glass

THE MUSEUM acquires relatively little ancient and Islamic glass. Nevertheless, five exceptional objects—three ancient and two Islamic—entered the collection in the 1990s. The earliest of these objects (1) is a mosaic glass inlay in the form of a collar. It was made in Egypt between about 300 and 50 B.C., when the country was ruled by descendants of Ptolemy, one of Alexander the Great's generals. Ptolemy and his successors introduced Greek culture to Egypt, and the collar contains both traditional Egyptian motifs (such as cobras) and classical elements (such as honeysuckle flowers in the top row of cane slices). The next object (2) is a bottle of the first century B.C., made of colorless and deep blue elements that were cast separately, then assembled and fused. The bottle was finished by grinding and polishing. No precise parallel for the form is known in glass, although similar vessels, also of deep blue and colorless glass, are in the British Museum and the archeological museum at Nicosia, Cyprus. The last ancient object presented here (3) is a medallion made in the third century A.D. It is decorated with a portrait of a woman drawn and painted on gold leaf sandwiched between two fused layers of glass. Fewer than 20 such medallions are known to exist, and, to the best of our knowledge, this was the only one that remained in private hands. In other words, when the owner decided to sell (and the French government granted an export license), it was a case of now or never. Thanks to the Clara S. Peck Endowment, we were able to acquire the object.

The first significant Islamic acquisition (4) is a conical cup that was intended to be held in the hand. The stained or luster decoration consists of a bird and five fish. The technique of painting glass with metallic stain seems to have been developed in Egypt not later than the eighth century, and our cup was probably made between the eighth and 11th centuries.

The second major Islamic acquisition (5) is a richly decorated candlestick. It dates from the 14th century, when the art of gilding and enameling on glass reached one of its highest points, in the Near East. A lengthy gilded inscription around the base may identify the original owner as Sultan al-Mansur Mohammed, who reigned in Damascus from 1361 to 1363.

Ptolemaic and Late Hellenistic Glass
———— 300–1 B.C. ————

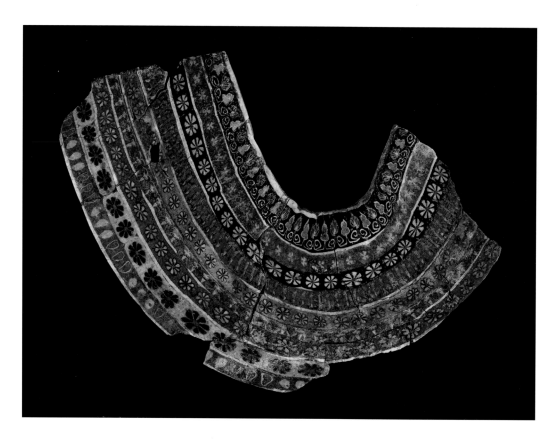

1. Inlay in the form of a collar, probably worn by a figure in a bas-relief, canes cut into slices, assembled, fused, and polished. Egypt, Ptolemaic, about 300–50 B.C. W. 17.0 cm (94.1.1).

2. Perfume or unguent bottle, cast, ground, polished, assembled, and fused. Probably eastern Mediterranean, first century B.C. H. 21.5 cm (98.1.97).

Roman and Early Islamic Glass
—— A.D. 200–1000 ——

3. Medallion with portrait, gold foil and pigment between two fused layers of glass, probably cast and ground. Roman Empire, perhaps Italy, third century A.D. D. 4.8 cm (90.1.3). Purchased with the assistance of Clara S. Peck Endowment.

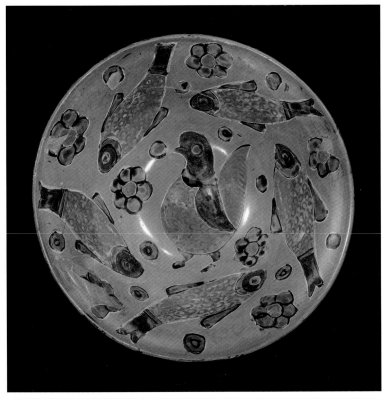

4. Conical cup, blown and stained. Islamic, probably Egypt, about 10th century. D. 15.8 cm (99.1.1). Gift of Lyuba and Ernesto Wolf.

Islamic Glass
—— 13TH OR 14TH CENTURY ——

5. Candlestick, blown, gilded, and enameled. Syria, late 13th or 14th century. H. 22.2 cm (90.1.1).

European Glass

FOR ADMINISTRATIVE PURPOSES, the Museum defines its collection of European glass as consisting mainly of objects made in Europe between the rise of Venice in the 15th century and the emergence of the Art Nouveau style in 1875. From the beginning, the collection has included exceptional objects. Over the years, curators expanded our holdings, building a collection distinguished equally by its scope and its depth. By 1990, therefore, the Museum's collection of European glass was unusually strong, without equal in the Western Hemisphere and arguably among the most comprehensive in the world.

Our collection-building tasks in the 1990s, therefore, were to fill gaps and, above all, to acquire objects of outstanding quality or historical significance. This was a challenging assignment, not least because any museum's acquisition strategy is at the mercy of chance. Who knows what may become available tomorrow? Perforce, curators are opportunists.

These are some of the key acquisitions of European glass in the last decade: (10) a miniature lampworked "diorama" depicting the story of Diana and Actaeon, probably made at Hall in Tyrol in the early 17th century; (11) four majestic covered goblets, each 44 cm high, probably made in Silesia about 1710 and engraved with personifications of Europe, Africa, America, and Asia; (12) a large cast medallion of King Louis XIV, made about 1675–1685 and attributed to Bernard Perrot; and (13) a covered goblet exquisitely engraved in Amsterdam by Jacob Sang in 1759.

Other notable additions to the collection include: (19) a massive cased and cut vase made at the Imperial Glassworks in St. Petersburg, Russia, about 1829; (27) the Saint-Louis "Gingham" paperweight of 1845–1855; and (42–44) lighting devices made by F. & C. Osler of Birmingham, England, between 1860 and 1890.

Finally, we were fortunate to acquire—by gift, bequest, and purchase—an exceptionally rich selection of 19th-century English cameo glass from the collection of the late Dr. and Mrs. Leonard S. Rakow. The acquisitions from the Rakow Collection included the replicas of the Portland Vase carved by John Northwood and Joseph Locke (page 8) and many of the most celebrated Woodall cameos, such as *Moorish Bathers* (48) and *The Great Tazza* (49).

Europe
1550–1710

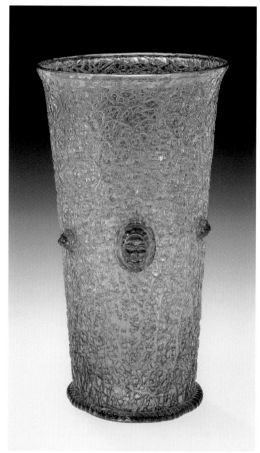

OPPOSITE, CLOCKWISE FROM TOP LEFT:
6. Covered two-handled bowl, blown and diamond-point engraved. Probably Italy, Venice (Murano), mid-16th century. OH. 26.1 cm (91.3.32). Gift of Ruth Blumka in memory of her daughter, Victoria.

7. Ice glass beaker, *façon de Venise*, blown, stamped, applied, and gilded. Low Countries, early 17th century. H. 22.4 cm (98.3.60).

8. Comet beaker (*kometenbeker*). Southern Netherlands, first half of the 17th century. H. 8.8 cm (95.3.43).

9. Hexagonal beaker, mold-blown, with applied rings. Germany, 17th century. H. 8.0 cm (95.3.40).

ABOVE:
10. Lampworked scene depicting Diana and Actaeon. Probably Austria, Hall in Tyrol, early 17th century. H. 21.8 cm (99.3.4).

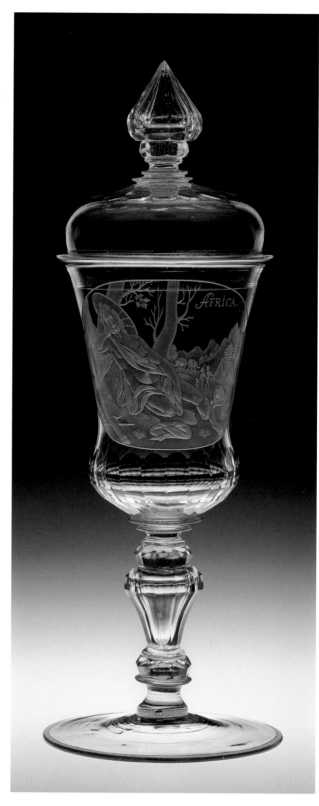

11. Set of four covered goblets engraved with personifications of Europe, Africa, America, and Asia. Probably Silesia, about 1710. OH. 44.0 cm (99.3.37).

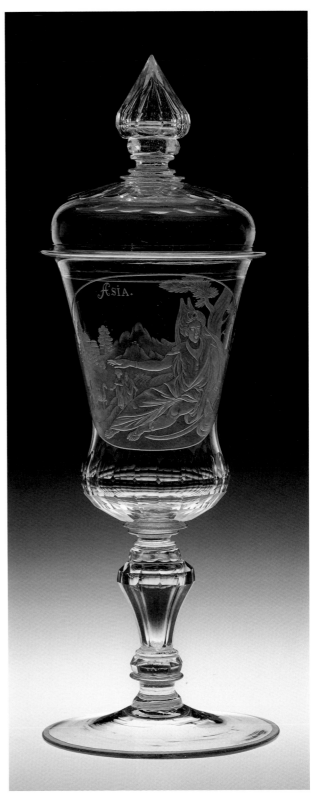

France
1675–1685

12. Medallion of King Louis XIV (r. 1643–1715), cast and gilded. Orléans, attributed to Bernard Perrot, about 1675–1685. H. (frame) 38.7 cm (99.3.2).

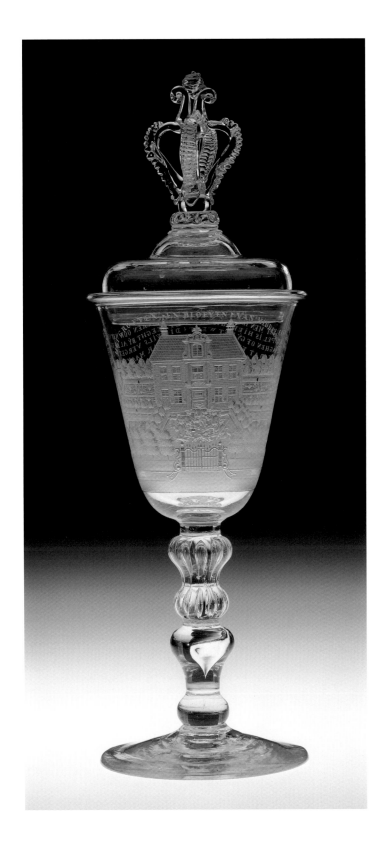

13. Covered goblet showing the country estate at Middelwyk near Soest, the Netherlands, copper-wheel engraved. Amsterdam, Jacob Sang (signed), 1759. OH. 35.4 cm (94.3.153).

Sweden
—— 1720–1730 ——

14. Reverse-painted mirror, enameled, gilded, and mercury-coated glass panels; carved, gessoed, and gilded wood frame. Stockholm, probably workshop of Christian and Gustaf Precht, 1720–1730. H. 145.0 cm (98.3.18).

Italy
1866–1907

15. Chandelier with six arms, blown, mold-blown, applied, and assembled; metal, foil, and wood. Venice, Salviati & C., about 1870. OH. 87.0 cm (98.3.8).

16. Top of a mosaic gueridon, white marble inlaid with ancient Roman mosaic glass, combined with 19th-century monochrome glass. Rome, probably Giovanni Rossignani, about 1866. D. 76.0 cm (97.3.10).

OPPOSITE
TOP:
17. Micromosaic panel depicting a benediction by Pope Leo XIII in St. Peter's Square, Rome, framed. Rome, Vatican Mosaic Workshop, Biagio P. Barzotti (signed), 1879. H. (frame) 48.5 cm (95.3.16).

BOTTOM:
18. Micromosaic panel depicting the basilica of San Marco, Venice, and its piazza. Venice, E. Cerato (signed), dated 1907. H. (frame) 152.8 cm (96.3.36). Gift of Dorothy and Charles J. Plohn Jr.

Russia
——— 1829–1900 ———

19. Vase, blown, overlaid, applied, cut, polished, cast, gilded, and assembled. St. Petersburg, Imperial Glassworks, about 1829. H. 56.0 cm (96.3.22).

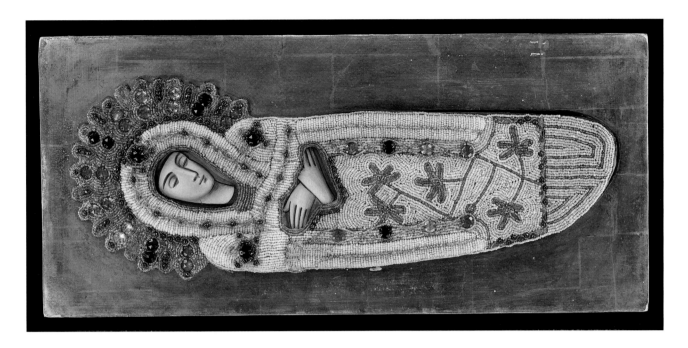

20. Beaded icon after the Tikhvin Madonna, Venetian glass beads, mother-of-pearl, embroidery, and gilded wood. Late 19th century. L. 52.6 cm (97.3.76).

21. Footed bowl, blown, applied, gilded, and enameled. St. Petersburg, Imperial Glassworks, dated 1863. H. 19.5 cm, D. (rim) 18.5 cm (98.3.62).

22. Vase, silver-gilt, enameled, and plique-à-jour. Moscow, workshop of Pavel Ovchinnikov, about 1900. H. 13.5 cm (94.3.92).

Bohemia and Germany
—— 1845–1890 ——

<small>CLOCKWISE FROM TOP LEFT:</small>

23. Covered goblet with a view of "Das Capitol zu Washington," blown, cased, cut, and engraved. Bohemia, made for the American market, about 1845–1855. OH. 38.4 cm, D. (cover) 15.7 cm (93.3.58).

24. Covered goblet with a view of "THE NEW CAPITOL WASHINGTON," blown, cut, stained, and engraved. Bohemia, made for the American market, about 1856–1857. OH. 50.1 cm, D. (cover) 18.0 cm (93.3.20).

25. Goblet with baluster stem, engraved in *Tiefschnitt* after a self-portrait of Rembrandt and his wife Saskia. Germany, engraved and signed by Franz Paul Zach, about 1860. H. 24.6 cm (93.3.59).

26. Pair of pedestal vases, mold-blown, applied, gilded, enameled, cut, and polished. Bohemia, Carlsbad, Ludwig Moser, about 1880–1890. H. (taller) 79.8 cm (96.3.16).

Paperweights and Related Objects
1845–1880

27. "Gingham" encased overlay paperweight. France, Saint-Louis, 1845–1855. D. 8.0 cm (95.3.62). Houghton Endowment.

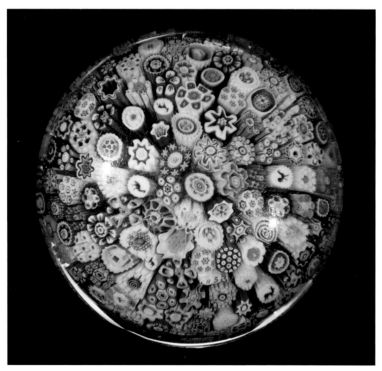

28. Paperweight, encased closely packed millefiori canes. France, Compagnie des Cristalleries de Baccarat, dated 1853. D. 7.4 cm (90.3.41). Gift of the Hon. and Mrs. Amory Houghton.

29. Macédoine egg-shaped hand cooler, assembled from cane slices, cut, molded, ground, and polished. France, Saint-Louis (signed "SL"), dated 1845. L. 6.4 cm (95.3.13).

30. Paperweight decorated with a pear on a red background, lampworked, assembled, encased, ground, and polished. France or Bohemia, mid-19th century. D. 7.6 cm (95.3.14).

31. Rose paperweight, lampworked. Probably Pantin factory near Paris, France, about 1880. D. 8.0 cm (91.3.92). Gift of Mrs. R. Henry Norweb Jr. in memory of the Hon. R. Henry Norweb.

32. Pair of candlesticks with lampworked floral bouquets, blown and cut. Probably Russia, St. Petersburg, about 1880. H. 22.4 cm (91.3.42). Gift of Mrs. George Ingham in memory of her husband.

England
1760–1900

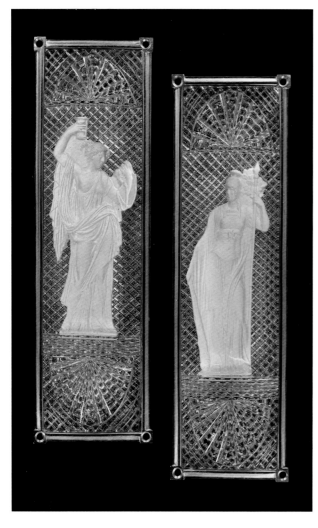

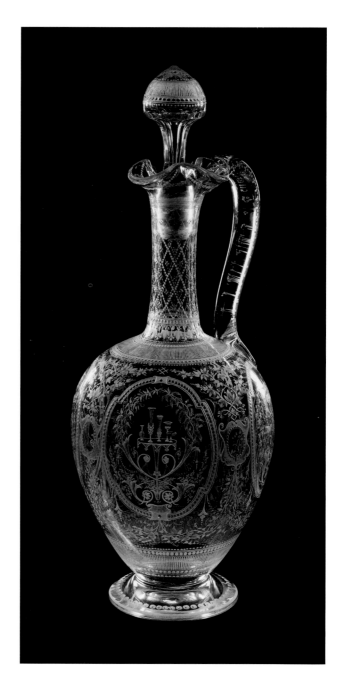

33. Vase, blown and enameled. Probably London, about 1760–1765. H. 13.4 cm (91.2.5). Gift of Mrs. John Mayer in memory of her husband.

34. Two door plates with figures of Temperance and Fortitude, pressed glass, molded sulphides, and brass frames. London, Falcon Glassworks of Apsley Pellatt, about 1830. H. 25.3 cm (93.2.2).

35. Carafe and stopper, blown and engraved. London, Falcon Glassworks of Pellatt and Co. (signed "Pellatt"), about 1862. H. 30.4 cm (97.2.8).

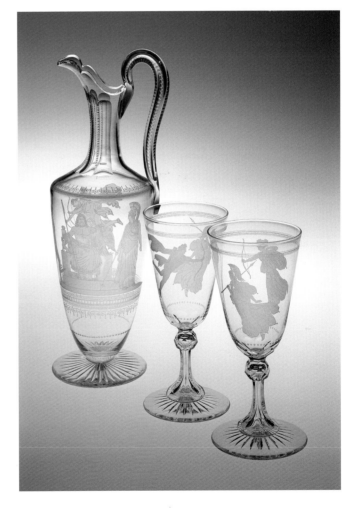

36. Miniature tea and coffee set, blown, applied, cut, and polished. About 1785. H. (tallest) 7.8 cm (98.2.1).

37. Water jug, blown and enameled. Wordsley, W. H., B. & J. Richardson, designed by Richard Redgrave, about 1850. H. 24.2 cm (97.2.18).

38. Claret jug and two glasses, blown, cut, polished, engraved, and acid-etched. Birmingham, F. & C. Osler, acid-etched by J. & J. Northwood, about 1870. H. (jug) 32.5 cm (96.2.12). Gift of Mallett & Son (Antiques) Ltd.

39. Carafe, blown, cut, polished, engraved, and acid-etched. Birmingham, F. & C. Osler, about 1883. H. 27.0 cm (96.2.11). Gift of Mallett & Son (Antiques) Ltd.

40. "Rock crystal" bowl, blown and cut. Stourbridge, Stevens and Williams, engraved by John Orchard, about 1894. H. 9.3 cm (98.2.6).

41. Epergne, blown and applied; gilded metalwork. Stourbridge, Stevens and Williams, designed by Frederick Carder, about 1900. H. 19.3 cm (98.2.10).

English Lighting Devices
———— 1860–1890 ————

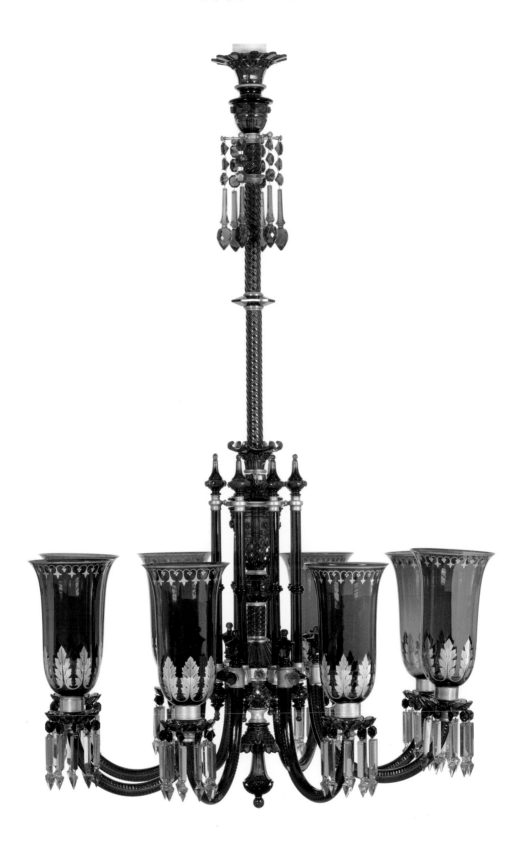

42. Chandelier with eight arms, blown, cut, and gilded; brass fittings. Birmingham, F. & C. Osler, about 1860–1880. H. 162.8 cm (95.2.13).

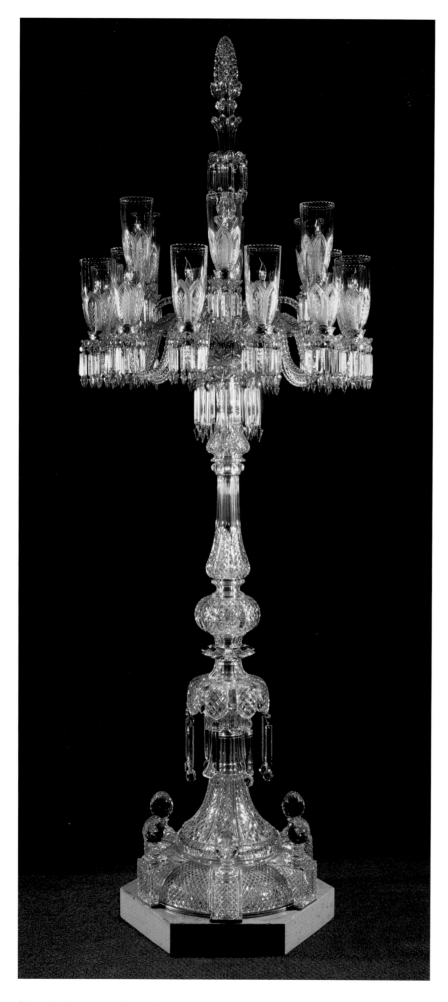

43. Candelabrum with 18 arms, blown and cut; white marble plinth. Birmingham, F. & C. Osler, about 1883. H. 295.0 cm (96.2.10).

44. Electrolier, blown and cut; brass fittings. Birmingham, F. & C. Osler, about 1887–1890. H. 94.0 cm (95.2.6).

English Cameo Glass
1878–1917

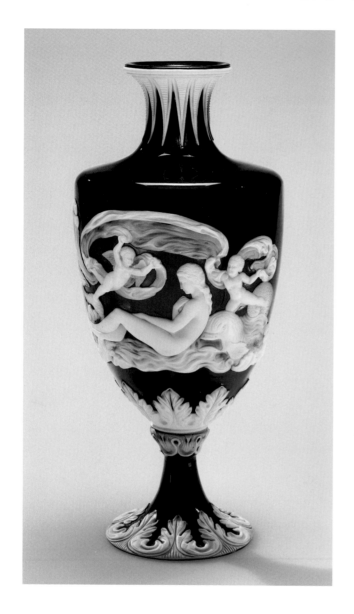

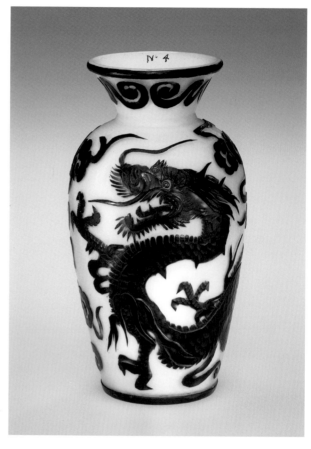

45. Vase, *The Birth of Venus*, blown, cased, acid-dipped, and carved. Stourbridge, carved by Alphonse Lechevral, about 1878, and later reworked by George Woodall. H. 28.5 cm (93.2.6).

46. Pair of medallions with portraits of Dr. and Mrs. Samuel Parkes Cadman, cast in two layers, acid-dipped, and engraved. Amblecote, Thomas Webb and Sons, engraved by George Woodall, about 1895. H. 15.7 cm (92.2.2). Gift of Mrs. Leonard S. Rakow.

47. Vase, "Nara" pattern, blown, cased, acid-dipped, and carved. Stourbridge, Stevens and Williams, engraved by Joshua Hodgetts, about 1917. H. 19.7 cm (98.2.7).

48. Plaque, *Moorish Bathers*, blown, cased, acid-dipped, carved, and engraved. Amblecote, Thomas Webb and Sons, carved and engraved by George Woodall, 1898. D. 46.3 cm (92.2.10). Bequest of Mrs. Leonard S. Rakow.

49. *The Great Tazza*, blown in two gathers, each gather cased four times and acid-dipped, carved, and engraved. Amblecote, Thomas Webb and Sons, decorated by George Woodall and his team, about 1889. H. 38.9 cm, D. 48.7 cm (92.2.8). Bequest of Mrs. Leonard S. Rakow.

American Glass

PRIDE OF PLACE among our acquisitions of early American glass in the 1990s goes to a diamond-daisy flask (50) attributed to the American Flint Glass Manufactory of Henry William Stiegel, which operated in Manheim, Pennsylvania, from 1769 to 1774. An even greater rarity is one-half of a brass mold for a liquor flask (52), which was given to the Museum by the late Gladys Richards and Paul Richards. The mold shows a portrait of the Marquis de Lafayette, and the inscriptions include the name "COVETRY/CT," identifying the mold as one used in the glassworks at Coventry, Connecticut. The Museum already owned a flask made from this mold. The back of the flask has the liberty cap and the initials "S. & S." The letters refer to Stebbins and Stebbins, a partnership that ran the factory in 1824–1825. Our mold, therefore, was made at this time. It is by far the earliest known example of a mold of this type. A third remarkable accession is a large cut and gilded vase (57) of colorless glass cased with three colored overlays. It was blown by William Leighton at the New England Glass Company between 1848 and 1858.

In 1997, as part of the renovation and expansion of the Museum, we decided to introduce a gallery devoted to the "Crystal City." This was the nickname given to Corning a century ago on account of its prominence as a producer of cut glass. With this in mind, we made a strenuous effort to enlarge our collection of cut glass made in Corning. Friends of the Museum played a major role in this effort, as the captions for the objects shown between pages 52 and 61 testify. The acquisitions in and after 1997 include examples from both large and smaller factories. Among the glass cut by J. Hoare and Company are a large centerpiece in the "Russian and Pillars" pattern (77), consisting of a bowl and an underplate made between 1882 and 1895, and a vase (81) that was cut in the "Monarch" pattern about 1890–1900. The glass cut by T. G. Hawkes and Company includes a rare "Venetian" vase with a greenish blue overlay (85) and an exceptional "Gravic Carnation" pitcher of 1909–1920 (92). Among the objects cut by O. F. Egginton and Company are an "Arabian" plate (96) and two "Berkshire" clarets or wineglasses (98), both made between 1896 and 1910. Giometti Brothers is represented by a large and elaborate electric lamp of about 1903–1920 (102).

American Glass
—— 1769–1875 ——

CLOCKWISE FROM TOP LEFT:

50. Diamond-daisy flask, mold-blown. Manheim, Pennsylvania, American Flint Glass Manufactory of Henry William Stiegel, 1769–1774. H. 10.8 cm (98.4.657). Gift of Dwight P. and Lorri Lanmon in honor of Julia Andrews Bissell.

51. Footed bowl, mold-blown and engraved, with molded panels around the base. Pittsburgh, Pennsylvania, Bakewell, Page and Bakewell, about 1815–1845. H. 16.2 cm (94.4.9).

52. Brass mold for liquor flask, showing portrait of the Marquis de Lafayette and inscribed "LAFAYETTE" and "COVETRY/CT," cast. Probably Coventry, Connecticut, 1824–1825. H. 20.1 cm (93.7.3). Gift of Gladys W. Richards and Paul C. Richards.

53. Footed bowl, blown three-mold, GIII-5 pattern. Sandwich, Massachusetts, Boston and Sandwich Glass Company, about 1825–1835. H. 13.3 cm (92.4.2).

57. Vase, blown, cased (four layers), cut, and gilded. Blown by William Leighton at the New England Glass Company, East Cambridge, Massachusetts, 1848–1858. H. 43.9 cm (93.4.9).

58. Goblet, blown, cased, and engraved with symbols of the Independent Order of Odd Fellows. East Cambridge, Massachusetts, New England Glass Company, about 1860–1870. Probably made for Charles Davis, son-in-law of Arthur Little Mitchell. H. 20.7 cm (94.4.159).

New England and New York
1830–1925

59. Vase, blown. East Cambridge, Massachusetts, New England Glass Company, about 1850. H. 23.7 cm (91.4.74). Gift of Sara Stedman Russell in memory of Isabel Leighton Hall.

60. Urn, blown and cut. New York, Christian Dorflinger's Long Island Flint Glass Works or Greenpoint Glass Works, about 1856–1865. H. 47.2 cm (91.4.77). Gift of Mr. and Mrs. Stephen Beers in memory of Isabel Dorflinger.

61. Soap dish, pressed. New England, probably Boston and Sandwich Glass Company or New England Glass Company, about 1830. OH. 8.0 cm (91.4.81). Gift of Samuel Schwartz in memory of Esther Ipp Schwartz.

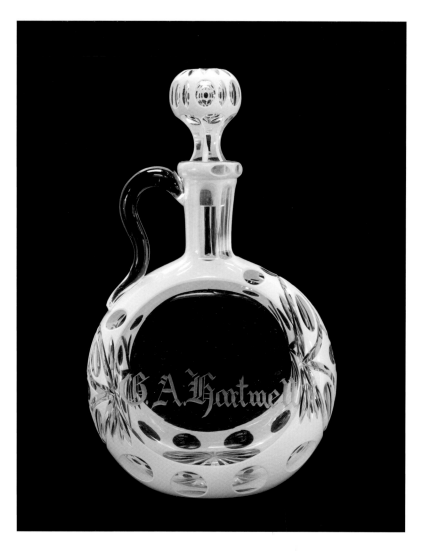

62. Whiskey jug, blown, cut, and engraved "G. A. Hartwell." Sandwich, Massachusetts, Boston and Sandwich Glass Company, about 1860–1875. OH. 23.5 cm (98.4.153). Gladys M. and Harry A. Snyder Memorial Trust.

BELOW LEFT:
63. Bowl, blown and cut. Probably Union Glass Company, Somerville, Massachusetts, or Pairpoint Corporation, New Bedford, Massachusetts, about 1900–1925. H. 12.6 cm (97.4.238). Gift of Harriet Smith.

BELOW:
64. Rose bowl, blown, cased, and cut. Meriden, Connecticut, cut by Gustave F. Ekdahl, 1909. H. 16.0 cm (98.4.169). Gift of Ada E. Ekdahl in memory of Felix J. Ekdahl.

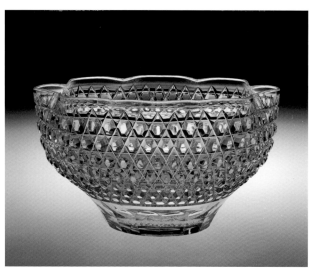

65. Sinumbra lamp, pressed, blown, tooled, and cut; metal parts fabricated by hand. East Cambridge, Massachusetts, New England Glass Company, about 1830–1835. H. 44.4 cm (96.4.139). Gertrude Christman Melvin Endowment.

66. Pair of lamps, blown, cased, and cut. East Cambridge, Massachusetts, New England Glass Company, 1855–1870. H. (taller) 24.6 cm (94.4.158).

67. Pair of lighting devices with pressed tripodal bases showing American eagles. New England Glass Company, East Cambridge, Massachusetts; South Boston Glass Company, Boston, Massachusetts; or Boston and Sandwich Glass Company, Sandwich, Massachusetts; probably 1830–1840. H. (larger) 42.9 cm (93.4.85).

68. Chamberstick, pressed. Sandwich, Massachusetts, Boston and Sandwich Glass Company, 1830–1840. H. 13.9 cm (96.4.187).

69. Burmese lamp with Coralene decoration, lead glass with some uranium, mold-blown and applied; brass and white metal. New Bedford, Massachusetts, Mt. Washington Glass Company, about 1885–1895. H. 45.2 cm (95.4.263).

New York, New Jersey, and Pennsylvania
1825–1915

OPPOSITE:

70. Pitcher, blown and cut. Jersey City, New Jersey, Jersey Glass Company, 1825–1845. H. 18.0 cm (98.4.168). Gift of Charles P. Whittemore.

71. Decanter, blown and cut. Probably Brooklyn Flint Glass Company, Brooklyn, New York, 1850–1855. H. 31.0 cm (96.4.191).

72. Fish trophy, made from pressed pickle dish, reverse-painted, mounted, and framed. Pittsburgh, Pennsylvania, Atterbury and Company, patented in 1872 (dish). H. 47.4 cm (94.4.121).

73. Wineglass from Centennial set, cut and engraved. White Mills, Pennsylvania, Christian Dorflinger's Wayne County Glass Works, 1876. H. 12.3 cm (92.4.122).

74. Compote, blown and cut. Pittsburgh, Pennsylvania, Bakewell, Pears and Company, 1876. D. 40.0 cm (91.4.13). Gift of Leila L. McKnight.

ABOVE LEFT:

75. Vase with silver rim, blown, cut, silver-chased, and engraved. Probably New York or Pennsylvania, about 1894. H. 39.5 cm (97.4.2). Bequest of Clementine Mills Schlaikjer and Jes Erich Schlaikjer.

ABOVE:

76. Electric lamp, mold-blown and cut with a pinwheel pattern; metal mounts cast and plated. Possibly Philadelphia, Pennsylvania, Quaker City Glass Company, or Meriden, Connecticut, J. D. Bergen and Company, about 1900–1915. H. 73.7 cm (96.4.157).

Corning, New York:
J. Hoare and Company
1882–1910

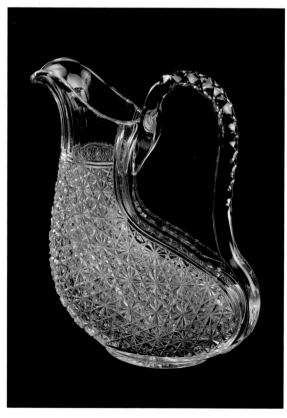

OPPOSITE:

77. Centerpiece bowl with underplate, "Russian and Pillars" pattern, blown and cut. Blank made at Corning Glass Works, cut at J. Hoare and Company, 1882–1895. L. 50.2 cm (99.4.92). Gift of Walter Poeth.

78. Wine pitcher, "Russian" pattern, blown, cut, and polished. Probably J. Hoare and Company, about 1882–1890. H. 22.2 cm (95.4.361). Gift of Harriet Smith.

79. Pair of cologne bottles, "Richelieu" pattern, blown, cut, and polished. Corning, New York, blown at Corning Glass Works and cut at J. Hoare and Company (glass); and New York, New York, Tiffany and Co. (silver); 1890–1895. OH. 20.1 cm (98.4.140). Gladys M. and Harry A. Snyder Memorial Trust.

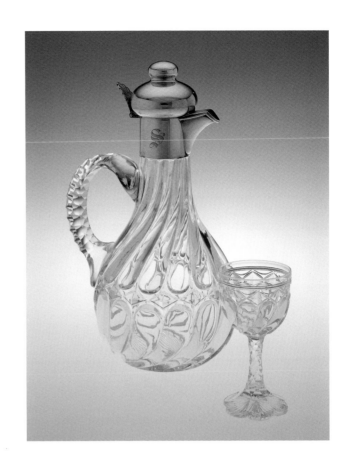

80. Claret jug and glass, "Twin City" pattern, blown, cut, and polished; silver mounts. About 1890–1900. H. (jug) 27.5 cm (96.4.51).

81. Vase, "Monarch" pattern, blown, cut, and polished. About 1890–1900. H. 30.2 cm (98.4.282). Gift of the Hamblen Trust of the Hamblen Family: Watt and Tallie Hamblen, Mary Margaret and Mattie Terry Hamblen.

82. Bowl, "Kohinoor" pattern, blown, cut, and polished. About 1910. D. 20.3 cm, H. 9.8 cm (98.4.643). Gift of Walter Poeth.

Corning, New York:
T. G. Hawkes and Company
1882–1939

Opposite:

83. Four wineglasses, "Persian" pattern, blown, cased, cut, and polished. 1882–1900. H. (tallest) 11.1 cm (98.4.278B, 280, 281, 279B). Gift of the Hamblen Trust of the Hamblen Family: Watt and Tallie Hamblen, Mary Margaret and Mattie Terry Hamblen.

84. Claret jug, "Venetian" pattern, blown, cased, and cut; silver mount made by Gorham Mfg. Co. About 1889–1899. H. 30.0 cm (99.4.94). Gift of Cliff and Ruth Jordan.

85. Vase, "Venetian" pattern, blown, cased, cut, and polished. Blank probably made at Corning Glass Works, about 1890–1900. H. 39.9 cm (97.4.22).

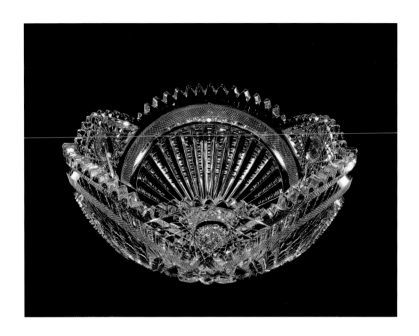

Top to bottom:

86. Bowl, "Nautilus" pattern, blown, cut, and polished. 1896–1901. D. 26.3 cm (95.4.364). Gift of Harriet Smith.

87. Bowl, "Napoleon" pattern, blown, cut, and polished. 1900–1910. D. 26.3 cm (95.4.362). Gift of Dorothy White Wehrstedt in memory of Norbert T. White.

88. Punch bowl, "Renaissance" pattern, blown, cut, engraved, and polished. Blank probably made at Steuben Glass Works, about 1903–1915. H. 20.4 cm (97.4.232).

89. Place setting, variant of Christian Dorflinger's "Centennial" pattern (three pieces—goblet, wine, and champagne—stamped with Hawkes's trademark), blown and cut, about 1900. H. (tallest) 16.9 cm (99.4.122A–E). Gift of Jim W. Miller in honor of his parents, Joe and Francis Miller.

90. Vase, "Rock Crystal" pattern, blown and engraved; base metal stand. Blank made at Steuben Glass Works and cut at T. G. Hawkes and Company, about 1903–1910. H. 39.2 cm (98.4.595).

91. Decanter and stopper, "Russian" pattern, blown, applied, cut, and polished. Blank probably made at Corning Glass Works, 1882–1895. OH. 28.2 cm (98.4.138). Purchased with the assistance of the Gladys M. and Harry A. Snyder Memorial Trust.

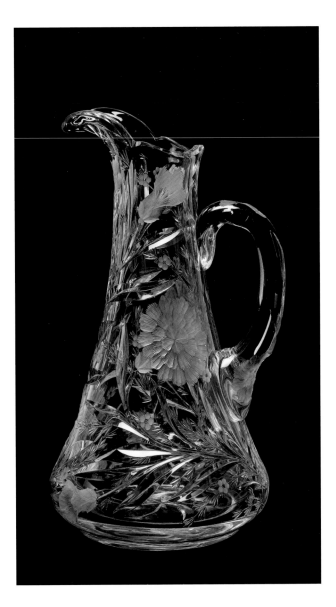

92. Pitcher, "Gravic Carnation" pattern, blown and engraved. 1909–1920. H. 28.2 cm (98.4.597). Gift of Harriet Smith.

93. Desk set (blotter with four glass corners, letter rack, two boxes with lids, pen tray, and inkwell), blown, cut, and engraved. 1915–1935. W. (blotter) 48.4 cm (96.4.185).

94. Vase, blown and engraved; silver base. Designed by Samuel Hawkes, 1939. H. 23.3 cm (98.4.9).

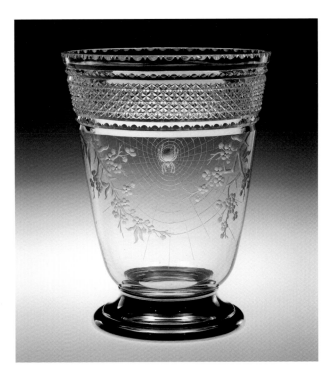

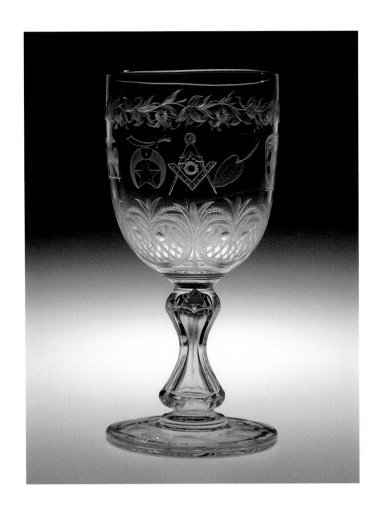

95. Goblet, blown and engraved with Masonic symbols. About 1900. H. 20.4 cm (98.4.291). Gift in memory of Bruce R. Gibbs, from his family.

96. Plate, "Arabian" pattern, blown, cut, and engraved. O. F. Egginton and Company, about 1896–1910. D. 18.0 cm (95.4.274). Gift of Mrs. Ruth L. Gay, granddaughter of Walter Egginton.

OPPOSITE:
97. Spoon tray, "Creswick" pattern, blown, cut, and polished. O. F. Egginton and Company, about 1896–1910. L. 20.2 cm (95.4.276). Gift of Mrs. Ruth L. Gay, granddaughter of Walter Egginton.

98. Two clarets or wineglasses, "Berkshire" pattern, blown, cut, and polished. O. F. Egginton and Company, about 1896–1910. H. (LEFT) 12.7 cm (95.4.277D, 278A). Gift of Mrs. Ruth L. Gay, granddaughter of Walter Egginton.

99. Decanter and stopper, "Rock Crystal" pattern, blown, engraved, and polished. Probably J. Hoare and Company or H. P. Sinclaire and Company, 1896–1915; possibly England. OH. 31.3 cm (97.4.233).

100. Shower vase, blown, cut, and polished; silver mount. Steuben Glass Works, designed by Frederick Carder, 1905–1913. H. 43.1 cm (97.4.21). Gift of Marvin S. Shadel in memory of Elizabeth Shadel.

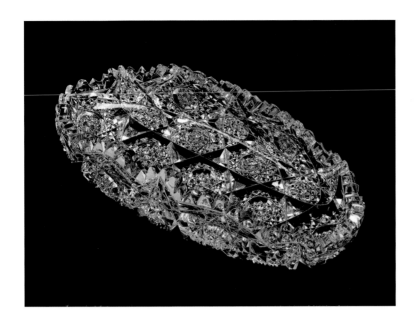

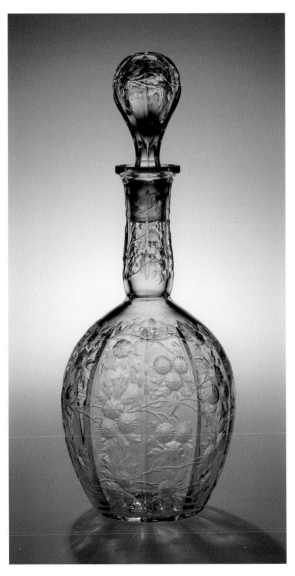

Corning and Elmira, New York
1899–1920

101. Punch bowl, blown and cut in pattern no. 17. Elmira, Elmira Cut Glass Company, 1899–1910. H. 27.4 cm (98.4.8).

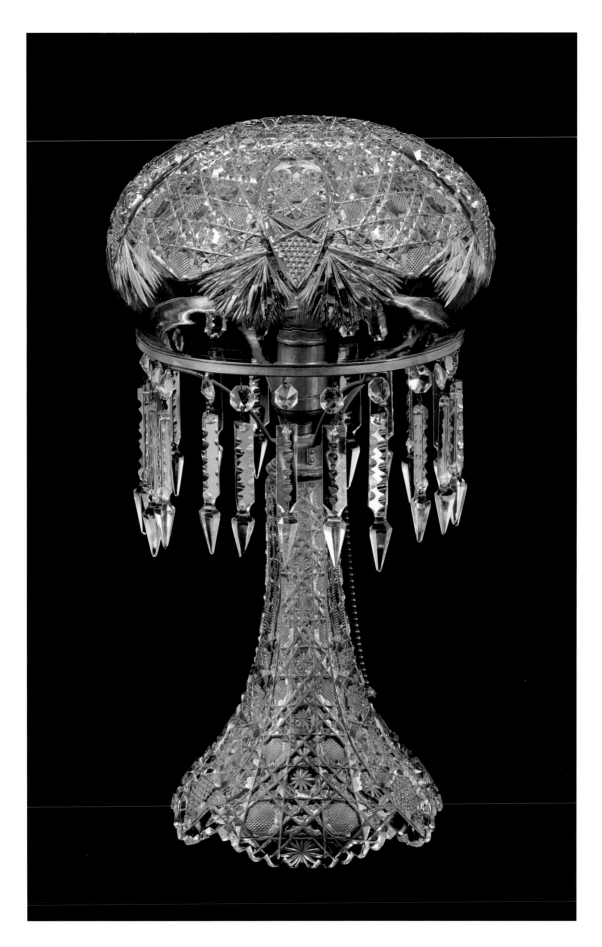

102. Electric lamp, blown, cut, and polished. Corning, Giometti Brothers, about 1903–1920. H. 45.8 cm (95.4.256). Gift of Mr. and Mrs. Matthew Cammen in memory of Attorney Claude V. Stowell, from his family.

American Cut Glass Company
—————— 1897–1914 ——————

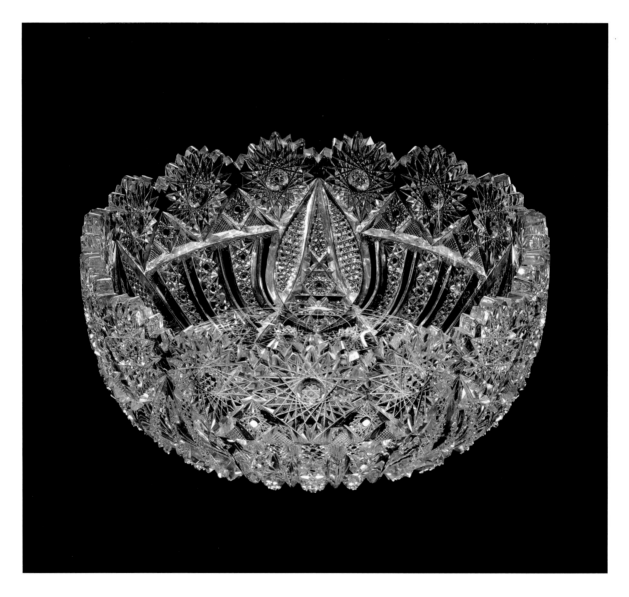

103. Bowl, blown and cut. Chicago, Illinois, or Lansing, Michigan, American Cut Glass
Company, designed by William C. Anderson, 1897–1914. D. 23.0 cm (99.4.77). Gift of
Robert Quaintance Fomon in memory of William C. Anderson, president and manager
of the American Cut Glass Company of Lansing, Michigan.

Art Nouveau to the Present

THE QUANTITY AND VARIETY of our acquisitions of glass made between the late 19th century and the present are such that the following notes barely scratch the surface.

We begin with two giants of Art Nouveau glassmaking: Louis Comfort Tiffany and Emile Gallé. The majestic vase (104) that was made for the 1893 world's fair in Chicago is among the earliest blown glass produced by the Tiffany Glass and Decorating Company in Corona, New York. The cranes and cloud scrolls reflect Tiffany's interest in Oriental art, which had a strong influence on many of his designs. *La Libellule*, or the Dragonfly Coupe (105), is an outstanding example of Gallé's genius for harnessing technical excellence to express his creativity. *La Libellule* was acquired jointly in 1980 by the Museum and Benedict Silverman (hence its accession number 80.3.59). In 1991, Mr. Silverman donated his half-interest in the coupe in memory of his wife, Gerry Lou Silverman.

A 20-year search ended in 1992 when the Museum acquired its first example of a window designed by Frank Lloyd Wright. The *Tree of Life* window (106) was designed in 1903–1904 for the Darwin D. Martin House in Buffalo, New York. The following year, we acquired a completely different window designed by Wright (107). The exuberant, asymmetric window from the Avery Coonley Playhouse in Riverside, Illinois, was designed about 1912.

Other acquisitions of glass made before World War II include several works by René Lalique (108, 109, 118, 119, and 121). One of these objects, a pendant (109), was acquired in 1990 on the assumption that it was designed by Lalique. This assumption was confirmed in 1994, when we purchased the original design (108) in a sale of drawings from the Lalique studio.

The Museum's holdings of glass made after World War II increased significantly in 1999, when The Steinberg Foundation donated 77 examples of original works of art and glass produced industrially in Czechoslovakia. This gift includes original works by René Roubíček (149), Adolf Matura (151), and Věra Lišková (153), and production glass designed by Stanislav Libenský in 1965 (150).

Finally, our interest in contemporary art and design continues unabated. Among the acquisitions of items made in the last decade are works by Dale Chihuly (178), Brian Clarke (144 and 145), Bernard Dejonghe (162), Franz X. Höller (167, pages 118 and 121), Libenský and Brychtová (157 and 159), Donald Lipski (176), Richard Meitner (168), Thomas Patti (179), and Toots Zynsky (181).

Louis Comfort Tiffany
1893

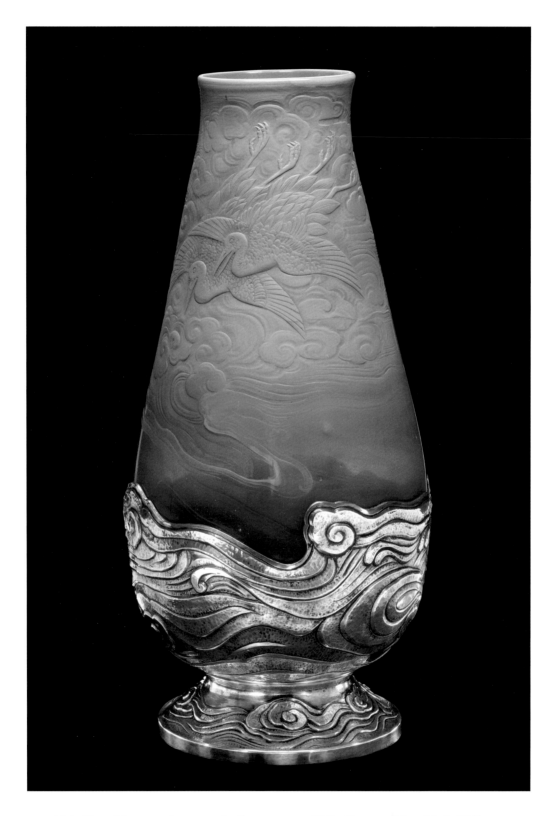

104. Vase, blown and engraved; silver mount. U.S., Corona, New York, Tiffany
Glass and Decorating Company, Louis Comfort Tiffany, mount dated 1893. H.
44.2 cm (98.4.24). Purchased with the assistance of the Houghton Endowment.

Emile Gallé
1903

105. Dragonfly Coupe, *La Libellule*, blown, layered, inlaid, and trailed glass with metal foil inclusions, cut and engraved. France, Emile Gallé, 1903. H. 18.3 cm (80.3.59). Gift in part of Benedict Silverman (1991) in memory of Gerry Lou Silverman.

Frank Lloyd Wright
1903–1912

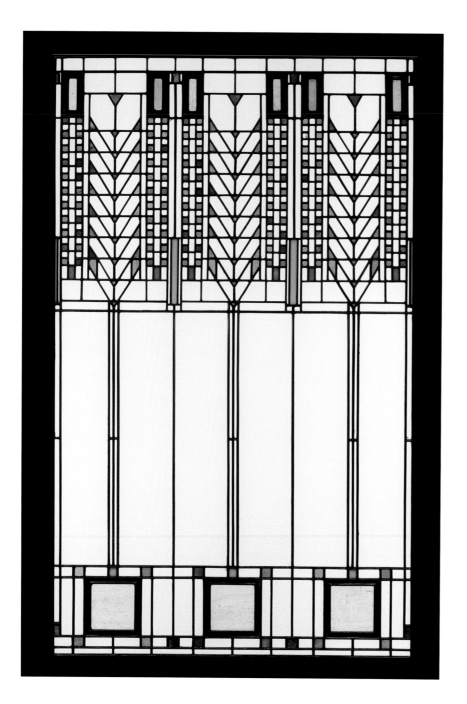

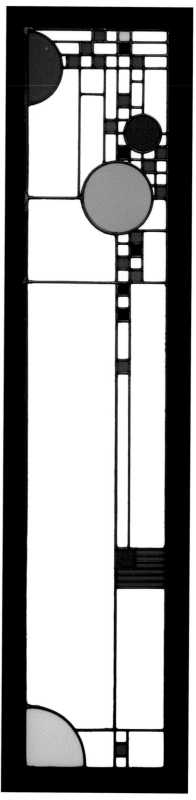

ABOVE:
106. Window, *Tree of Life*. U.S., designed by Frank Lloyd Wright for the Darwin D. Martin House, Buffalo, New York, 1903–1904. H. 100.9 cm (92.4.175). Clara S. Peck Endowment.

107. Window, cut glass assembled with zinc came. U.S., designed by Frank Lloyd Wright for the Avery Coonley Playhouse, Riverside, Illinois, about 1912. H. (frame) 175.7 cm (93.4.17). Clara S. Peck Endowment.

René Lalique
—— 1905 ——

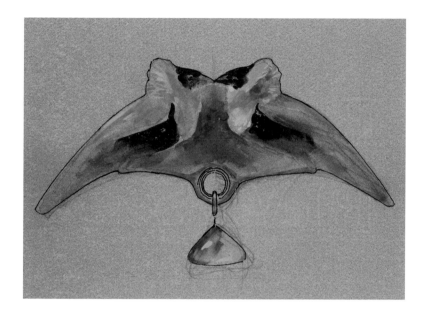

108. Preliminary study for pendant, pencil, ink, watercolor, and gouache on translucent Blanchet Frères Kléber paper (BFK-Rives watermark). France, studio of René Lalique, about 1905. H. 28.0 cm.

109. Pendant, colorless *pâte de verre* with spots of added color, copper and metal foil backing; copper, gold, and baroque pearl. France, René Lalique, about 1905. W. 11.3 cm (90.3.37).

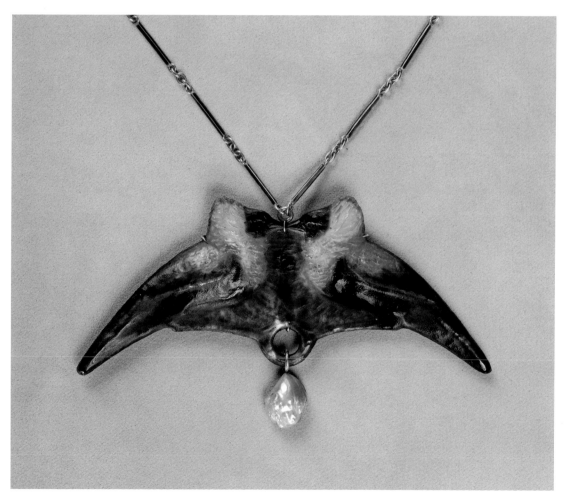

Whitefriars Glass Works
——— 1906 ———

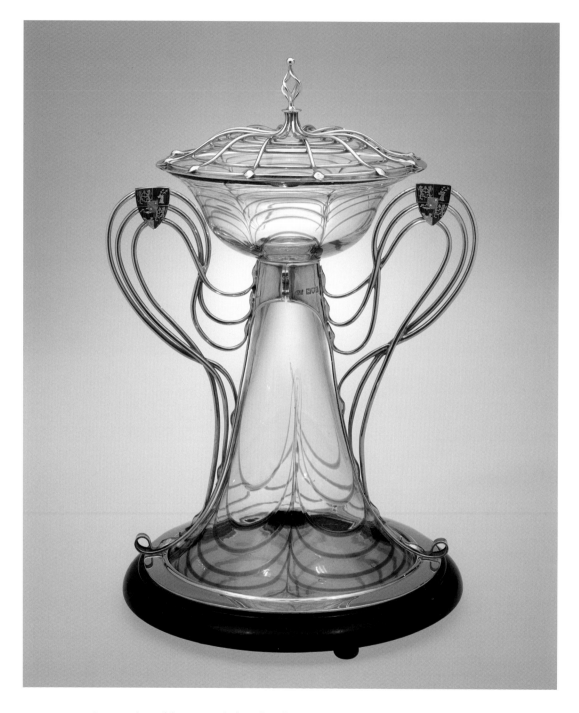

110. Centerpiece, blown, trailed and pulled decoration; wood and silver mounts, with enameled shields. England, James Powell and Sons, Whitefriars Glass Works, designed by Harry Powell, made for Count Minerbi, 1906. H. 27.0 cm (90.2.3). Gift of Alastair Duncan.

Umberto Bellotto

1914–1920

111. Sculptural vessel, blown,
picked-up shards and *murrine*,
wrought iron. Italy, Umberto
Bellotto, about 1914–1920. H.
65.6 cm (95.3.36).

Louis Comfort Tiffany and Tiffany Studios

1900–1914

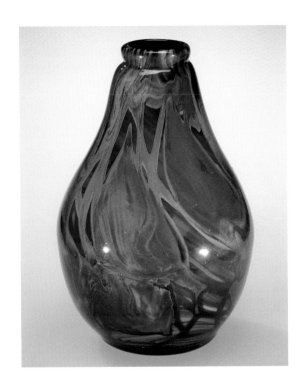

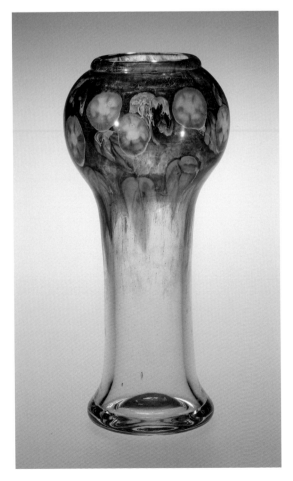

112. Reactive paperweight vase, blown, with encased metallic oxides. U.S., New York, New York, Tiffany Studios, about 1900–1908. H. 18.2 cm (94.4.174). Gift of Benedict Silverman.

113. Detail of window, *The Righteous Shall Receive a Crown of Glory*, various sheet glasses, cut, enameled, and assembled; hardwood frame. U.S., New York, New York, Tiffany Studios, about 1901. H. (detail) 144.8 cm (96.4.230). Gift of Bruce and Adele Randall.

114. Vase with morning-glory design, blown and encased. U.S., Louis Comfort Tiffany, about 1914. H. 24.9 cm (97.4.125). Gift of Mr. and Mrs. Howard Stein.

Sweden
1915–1937

TOP LEFT:
115. Vase, blown, cased, wheel-cut, and acid-etched. Orrefors Glasbruk, Heinrich Wollmann, Fritz Blomqvist, and Knut Bergqvist, about 1915–1916. H. 25.3 cm (98.3.49). Gift in part of Gerald M. Eggert in memory of Christine Clara Weiss.

LEFT:
116. Vase, blown and engraved. Orrefors Glasbruk, Viktor (Vicke) Emanuel Lindstrand, designed in 1935. H. 22.0 cm (98.3.31). Gift of Gerald M. Eggert in memory of Christine Clara Weiss.

ABOVE:
117. *Shark-Killer*, blown and engraved. Orrefors Glasbruk, designed by Viktor (Vicke) Emanuel Lindstrand, engraved by Emil Goldman, 1937. H. 32.4 cm (90.3.1). Gift of Arthur and Theresa Greenblatt.

France

1924–1947

118. Vase, *Serpent*, mold-blown and acid-etched. Lalique et Cie, designed by René Lalique, 1924. H. 24.8 cm (93.3.41).

119. Clock frame and stand, *Le Jour et la nuit*, pressed and acid-etched; silver stand. René Lalique, designed in 1926. H. 37.0 cm (96.3.10).

120. Vase with deeply modeled birds and foliage, on original glass plinth, cast, etched, cut, and carved. Aristide-Michel Colotte, 1927–1943. H. 35.6 cm (94.3.115).

121. Automobile hood ornament, *Victoire*, pressed. René Lalique, about 1928–1947. H. 15.8 cm (98.3.14).

122. Three bottles with stoppers, blown and acid-etched. Troyes, Maurice Marinot, about 1930–1935. H. (tallest) 26.5 cm (91.3.118, 116, 120). Gift of Mrs. Evangeline B. Bruce.

Europe
—— 1922–1952 ——

TOP LEFT:
123. Fluted vase, blown and molded. Czechoslovakia, Adolfov, Meyr's Neffe Glassworks/ Moser Glassworks, designed by Josef Hoffmann for the Wiener Werkstätte, Vienna, Austria, 1922–1931. H. 23.0 cm (97.3.9).

124. Teapot with cover and stand, sugar bowl with cover and stand, and creamer with stand, pressed. The Netherlands, Glasfabriek Leerdam, designed by Hendrik Petrus Berlage and Piet Zwart, 1924. H. (teapot) 14.2 cm (95.3.104, 105).

125. Vase for the dining room of the Savoy Hotel, Helsinki, blown in a wooden mold. Finland, Karhula Glassworks, designed by Alvar Aalto, 1936. H. 14.3 cm (97.3.62).

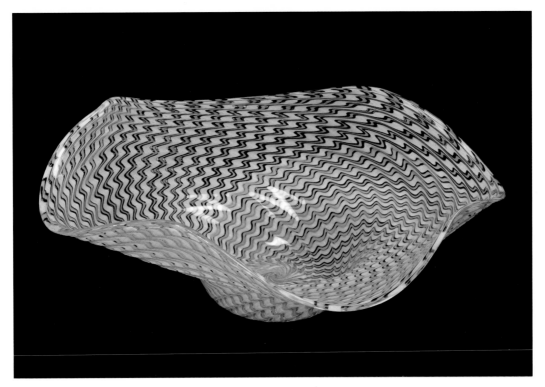

126. Ornamental set, blown and hot-worked. Italy, Vetri Soffiati Muranesi–Venini & C., designed by Napoleone Martinuzzi, about 1930. H. (tallest) 23.6 cm (96.3.20).

127. *A trina* (lace) bowl, applied and mold-blown. Italy, Murano, Vetri Decorativi Rag. Aureliano Toso, designed by Dino Martens, about 1952. D. 40.4 cm (98.3.59). Gift of Luis O. Barros.

United States
1915–1934

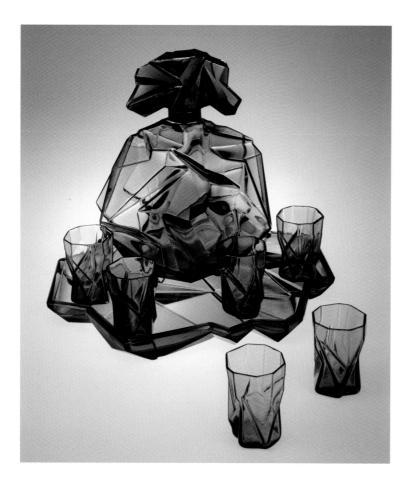

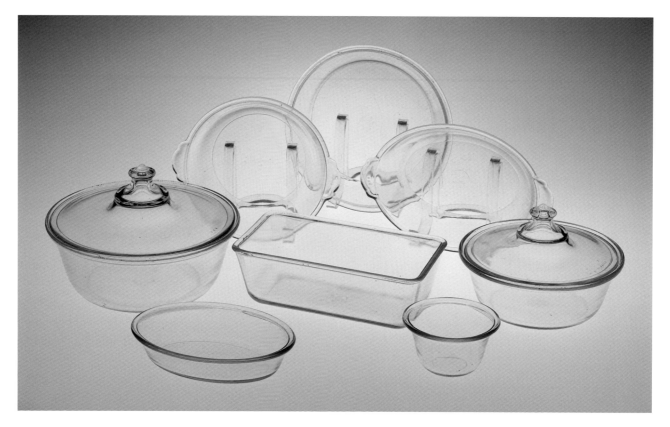

OPPOSITE:
128. "Ruba Rombic" liquor bottle, six whiskey glasses, and tray, mold-blown and pressed. Coraopolis, Pennsylvania, Consolidated Lamp and Glass Company, designed by Reuben Haley, 1928–1932. H. (bottle) 23.4 cm (92.4.121).

129. Examples from first marketed Pyrex® bakeware, pressed. Corning, New York, Corning Glass Works, 1915–1919. H. (tallest) 14.9 cm (96.4.167–175). Gift of Jerry E. Wright.

130. Intarsia vase. Corning, New York, designed by Frederick Carder, about 1929. H. 14.2 cm (94.4.175). Bequest of Paul V. Gardner.

ABOVE:
131. Light bulb tester/display in the shape of a light bulb, designed by Maxfield Parrish. Coshocton, Ohio, American Art Works Inc. for the Edison Mazda lamp division of the General Electric Company, 1924–1934. OH. 69.5 cm (95.4.261).

Beaded Objects
1920–1992

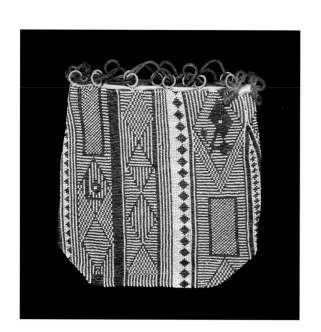

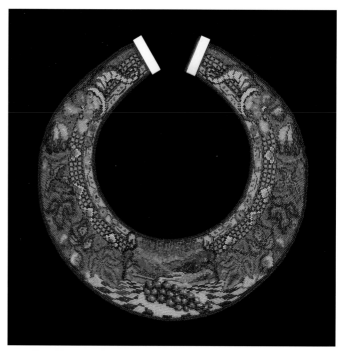

OPPOSITE:

132. Beaded handbag, glass beads, metallic thread cord, and silk lining. Austria, Vienna, Wiener Werkstätte, designed by Maria Likarz, 1920s. H. 18.3 cm (97.3.1).

133. Three covered wedding baskets, natural fibers, fabric, glass beads, and *hassa* shells. Indonesia, Sumatra, Lampung Bay area, probably 1930–1950. H. (tallest) 26.4 cm (97.6.1–3).

134. Beaded collar, *L'Automne*, antique glass seed beads knitted with silk thread. Germany, Natacha Wolters, 1989. D. 27.0 cm (97.3.29).

135. *Three Graces Oblivious while Los Angeles Burns*, blown; woven, knotted, and stitched glass beads; flameworked eyes. U.S., Joyce Scott, 1992. H. 53.8 cm (97.4.214).

Flat Glass
1952–1998

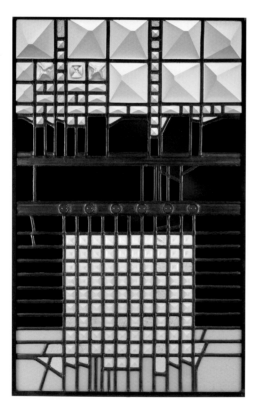

TOP TO BOTTOM:

141. Leaded glass panel, *Fish*. England, London, Theresa Obermayr Sowers, 1952. H. 41.2 cm (92.2.5). Gift of Judi Jordan Sowers.

142. Leaded glass panel, cut and assembled. Federal Republic of Germany, Ludwig Schaffrath, 1968. H. 90.4 cm (90.3.44). Bequest of Robert Sowers in memory of Theresa Obermayr Sowers.

143. Stained glass triptych, *Caught in a Flood* from the "Natural Disasters" series, cut, engraved, enameled, and assembled with copper foil. U.S., Judith Schaechter, 1990. L. 100.7 cm (91.4.23).

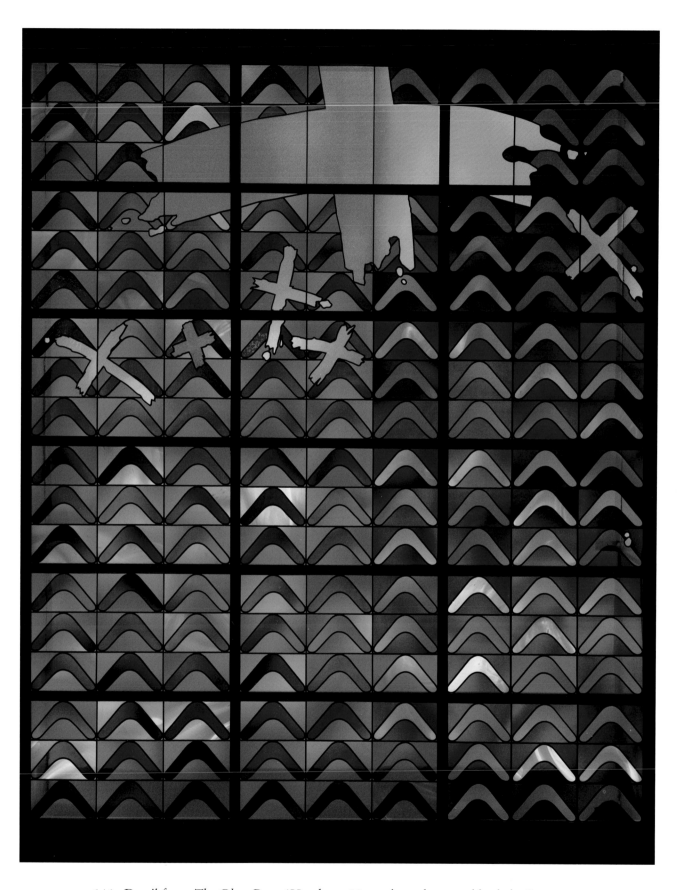

144. Detail from *The Glass Dune/Hamburg*, 18 panels, each cut and leaded. Germany, W. Derix Glass Studios, designed by Brian Clarke, 1992. H. (panel) 55.4 cm (95.3.32). Photo courtesy of Tony Shafrazi Gallery.

145. *The Glass Wall*, stained glass, aluminum, and steel cable. England, designed by Brian Clarke, glass manufactured at Franz Mayer, Munich, Germany, 1998. H. 6.3 m, L. 22.4 m (99.2.4). Photo by Fred Scruton, courtesy of Tony Shafrazi Gallery.

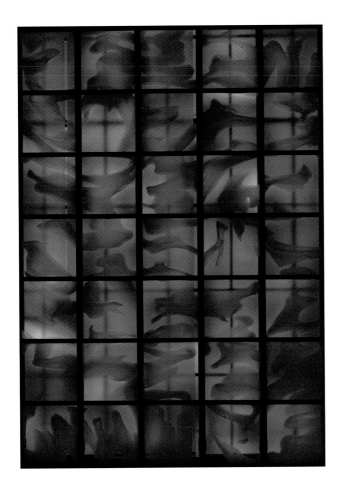

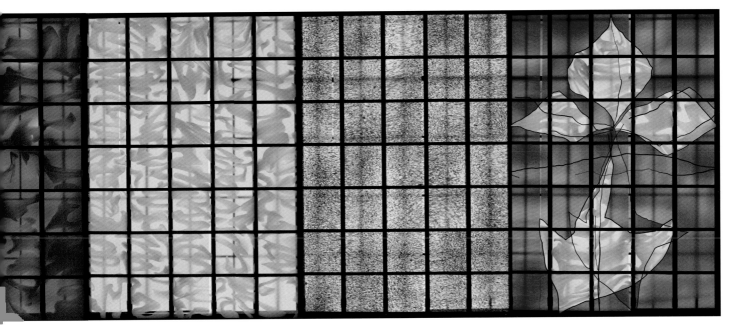

U.S.S.R.
1949–1970

146. Vase commemorating the 70th birthday of Joseph Stalin, mold-blown and acid-etched; silver and copper collar. Possibly Gus-Khrustalny or Leningrad Glassworks, possibly designed by Yevheny Ivanovich Rogov, 1949. H. 48.7 cm (95.3.25).

147. *Man, Horse, Dog, Bird*, blown, with hot applications. Probably Leningrad Art Glass Factory, Boris Alexandrovich Smirnov, about 1970. H. 35.3 cm (90.3.36).

Czechoslovakia

1960–1989

148. Flacon with stopper, blown and cut. Miroslav Platek, 1960. H. 14.6 cm (99.3.63). Gift of The Steinberg Foundation.

149. Bottle, blown and applied. René Roubíček, 1964. H. 20.6 cm (99.3.42). Gift of The Steinberg Foundation.

150. Pitcher and two beakers, blown and applied. Stanislav Libenský, 1965. H. (pitcher) 15.3 cm (99.3.46). Gift of The Steinberg Foundation.

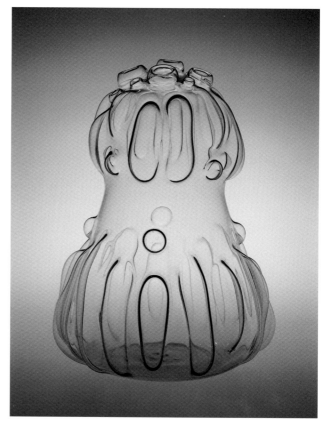

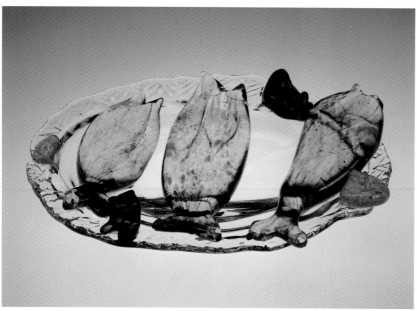

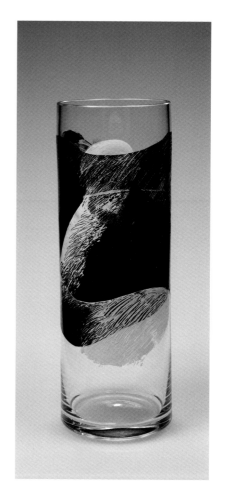

Top left:
151. Vase, blown. Adolf Matura, about 1965. H. 24.6 cm (99.3.53). Gift of The Steinberg Foundation.

152. *Homage to Palissy, Still Life with Fish*, slumped and applied. Miluše Roubíčková, 1968. L. 30.1 cm (99.3.61). Gift of The Steinberg Foundation.

Top right:
153. *Small Ikebana*, flameworked. Věra Lišková, 1970–1979. H. 33.6 cm (99.3.69). Gift of The Steinberg Foundation.

154. Vase, blown and enameled. Jan Adam, 1978. H. 32.5 cm (99.3.52). Gift of The Steinberg Foundation.

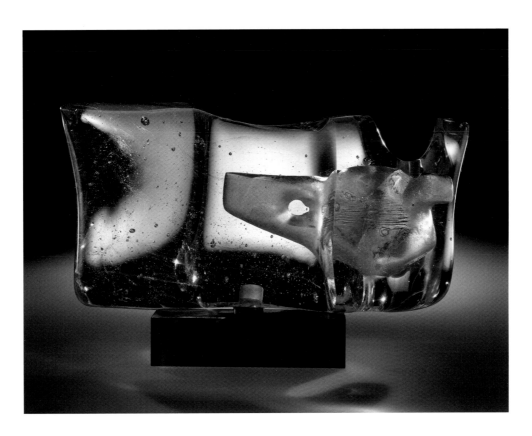

155. *The Inner Space*, glass melted in a mold; metal base. Jan Fišar, 1968.
H. 19.4 cm (97.3.58). Gift of the artist.

156. Sculpture, *Blackcoater*, glass melted in a mold, ground, and polished.
Ivan Mareš, 1989. H. 57.2 cm (92.3.12).

Czech Republic: Stanislav Libenský and Jaroslava Brychtová
1992–1993

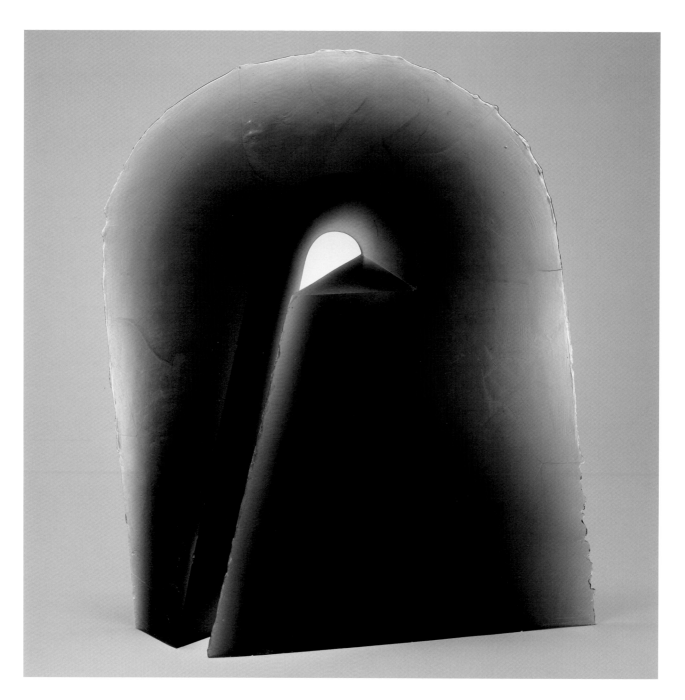

157. *Big Arcus/Arcus III*, glass melted in a mold. Stanislav Libenský and Jaroslava Brychtová, 1992–1993. H. 104.1 cm (93.3.26). Gift of the artists.

158. Preliminary study for *Red Pyramid*, charcoal and gouache on paper mounted on canvas. Stanislav Libenský, 1993. H. 104.1 cm (94.7.19). Gift of the artist and Jaroslava Brychtová.

159. *Red Pyramid*, glass melted in a mold. Stanislav Libenský and Jaroslava Brychtová, 1993. H. 83.9 cm (94.3.101). Gift of the artists. Photo by Gabriel Urbánek.

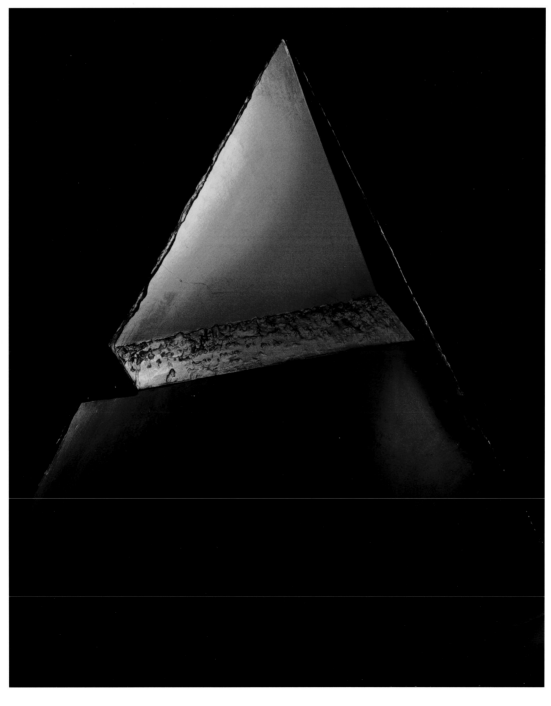

France
1992–1997

160. *La Poule, le singe et les oeufs* (The chicken, the monkey, and the eggs), reverse-painted. Gilles Duliscouet (Dulis), about 1992. H. 82.5 cm (97.3.73).

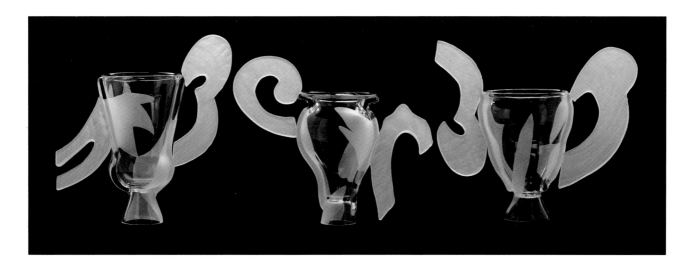

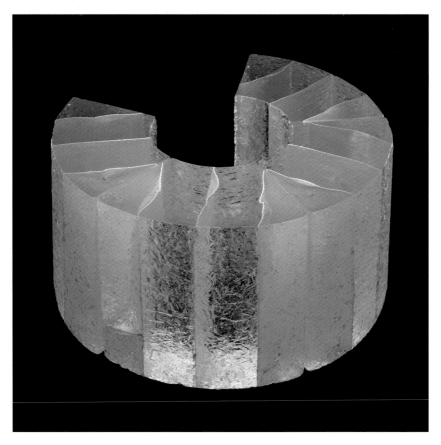

161. Sculpture, *Triptych B*, blown, applied, assembled, and sandblasted. Betty Woodman, 1993–1996. H. 52.5 cm (98.3.15). Gift of the Ben W. Heineman family.

162. *Small Circle*, optical glass slumped into molds and chiseled. Bernard Dejonghe, 1997. H. 30.0 cm (97.3.72). Gift of the Ben W. Heineman family.

Italy
—— 1993–1996 ——

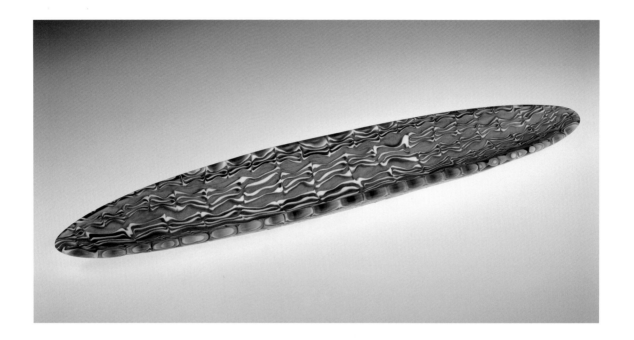

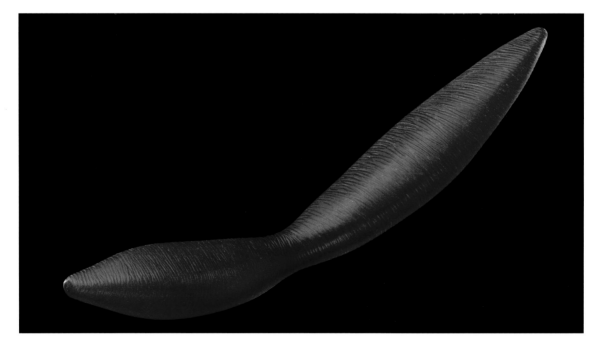

TOP:
163. *Nile*, fused *murrine* slumped over a mold and stone wheel-carved. Laura de Santillana, 1996. L. 72.8 cm (97.3.25).

164. *Custodi di sabbia*, blown and ground. Alessandro Diaz de Santillana with the assistance of Pino Signoretto, 1993. H. 25.8 cm (95.3.31).

Germany and Switzerland
1968–1996

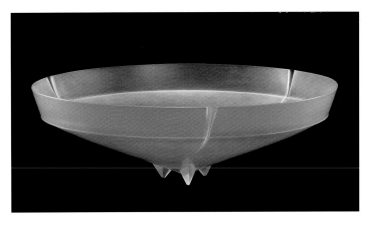

165. Sculpture, blown, applied, and tooled. Germany, Erwin Eisch, 1968. H. 67.5 cm (98.3.11). Gift of the artist.

166. *Red and Blue Sentinel* and *Red and Blue Top*, blown, cased, and cut. Switzerland, Monica Guggisberg and Philip Baldwin, 1996. H. (taller) 47.4 cm (97.3.33, 34).

167. Bowl, blown and cut. Germany, Franz X. Höller, 1996. D. 40.3 cm (97.3.36).

The Netherlands
1994

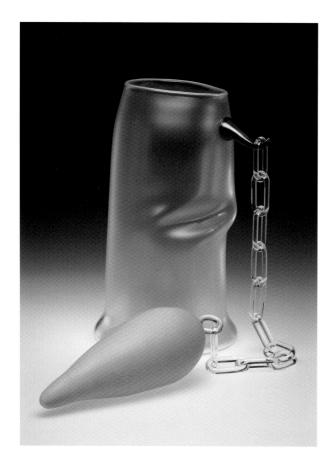

168. *Wisdom*, blown, tooled, acid-etched, flameworked, enameled, and iridized. Richard Meitner, 1994. H. 37.8 cm (95.3.47).

169. *Spiral Forms*, window glass, sagged and assembled. Bert Frijns, 1994. H. 50.0 cm (95.3.76).

Australia and Japan
1994–1995

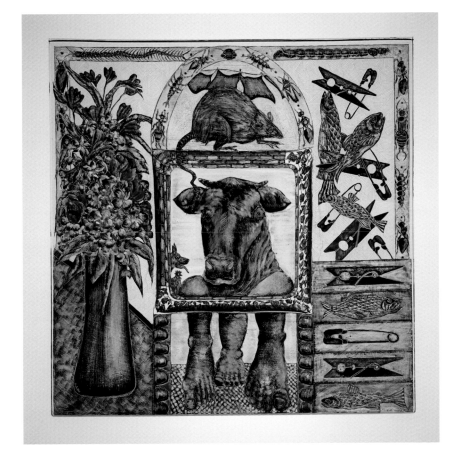

170. *One Step Forward, Two Steps Back*, slumped and reverse-enameled. Australia, Deb Cocks, 1994. H. 50.3 cm (95.6.12).

171. *Mizuno Utsuwa* (Water vessel), sheet glass, cut, laminated, ground, and polished. Japan, Toshio Iezumi, 1995. D. 60.9 cm (95.6.15). Purchased with the assistance of Daniel Greenberg and Susan Steinhauser.

United States

1960–1997

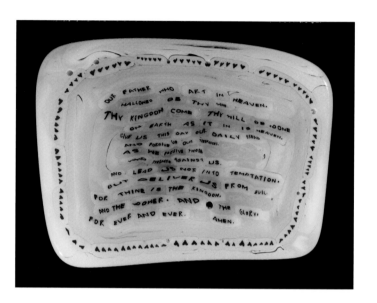

172. Necklace, *Space*, fused glass and ceramic "stones"; sterling silver mount. Elsa Freund, 1960. L. 19.5 cm (91.4.17). Gift of Jane Hershey.

173. *Murrina* containing the entire text of the Lord's Prayer, assembled, fused, reheated, and pulled. Richard Marquis, 1970. H. 1.7 cm (94.4.111A). Gift of the artist.

174. *Window Seat #1*, acid-etched window glass and welded steel. Bruce Chao, 1987. H. 110.0 cm (92.4.149).

175. *Home Again, Eat Again, Watch Some TV*, blown, cut, etched, engraved, and assembled glass; mixed media. Richard "Rick" Bernstein, 1983. OH. 140.0 cm (91.4.54). Gift of Anne and Ronald Abramson.

176. *Water Lilies #52.* Donald Lipski, 1990. H. 29.0 cm (92.4.5). Gift of Maureen and Roger Ackerman.

177. Wall panel, *Window Bkd #6*, layered sheet glass, deposited Incomel and silicon monoxide, wood, and fabric. Larry Bell, 1992. H. 135.2 cm (94.4.146).

178. *Cadmium Yellow-Orange Venetian #398*, blown and iridized, with hot applications and gold leaf. Dale Chihuly, 1990. H. 49.0 cm (90.4.129). Gift of Mr. and Mrs. James R. Houghton.

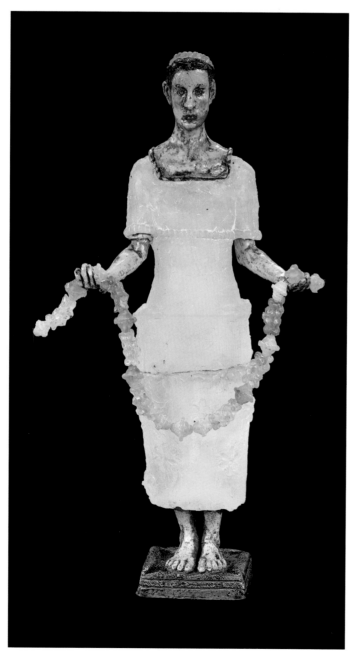

179. Sculpture, *Clear Lumina with Azurlite*, fused and shaped while hot. Thomas Patti, 1992. H. 10.3 cm (94.4.1). Purchased with funds from the Art Alliance for Contemporary Glass, the Creative Glass Center of America, Ben W. Heineman Sr., and Carl H. Pforzheimer III.

180. *Jump*, glass fused in molds and raku-fired ceramic. Judy Hill, 1993. H. 51.1 cm (95.4.1).

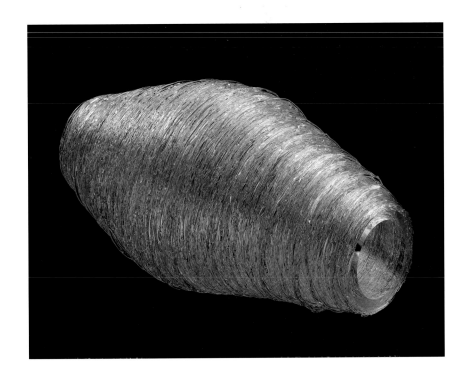

181. *Water Spout #13*, blown and hot-worked. Toots Zynsky with the assistance of Richard Royal, 1994. L. 24.3 cm (95.4.27).

182. *Piano*, glass mosaic over charcoal on Masonite®. Robert Kehlmann, 1994. W. 73.8 cm (96.4.57).

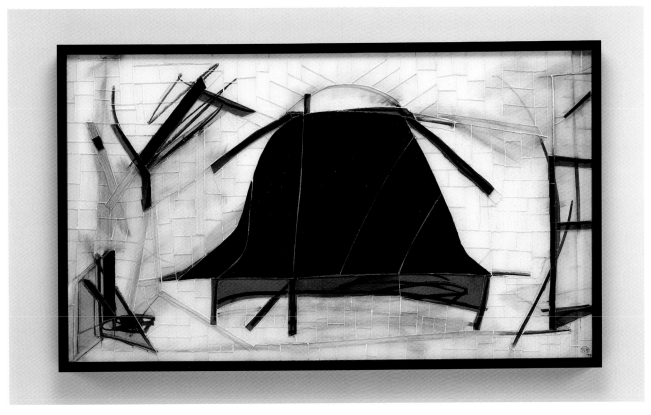

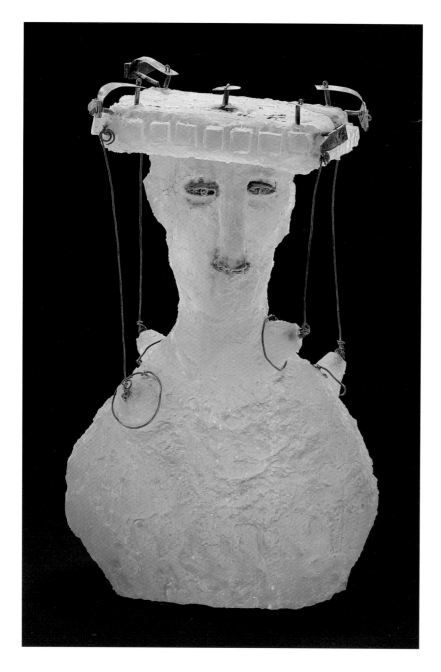

183. *Bust with Locator*, cast and sandblasted; patinated metal. Hank Murta Adams, 1995. H. 73.6 cm (96.4.1).

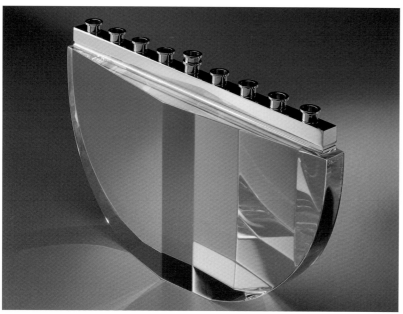

184. *Menorah*, cast, cut, and polished; silver-plated metal. Corning, New York, Steuben, designed by Joel A. Smith in 1992, made in 1995. H. 13.9 cm, W. 24.5 cm (95.4.258). Gift of Steuben and the designer.

185. Vase, *Aurora*, tesserae (mosaic) technique, fused and blown. Dorothy Hafner with the assistance of Lino Tagliapietra, 1995. H. 47.3 cm (98.4.133). Gift of Martin Bresler.

186. Platter from "Colorways" series, slumped and fused. Dorothy Hafner, 1997. D. 33.6 cm (98.4.135). Gift of the artist.

187. Reverse painting, *Corning Glassworks 50th Anniversary Celebration*, glass, acrylic, paint, ink, and foil; wood frame. Stratford, Connecticut, Milton W. Bond, 1996. H. 85.1 cm (97.4.3).

The Rakow Commissions

THE RAKOW COMMISSION is awarded annually by The Corning Museum of Glass. This program was established to encourage fine glassmaking and the development of new works of art in glass by awarding commissions to individual artists who show great promise. It is intended to permit glassmakers to venture into new areas that they might otherwise be unable to explore because of financial limitations. In recent years, the scope of the commission has been expanded to include the work of established artists. Each commissioned work enters the Museum's collection and is exhibited on its own for one year before it is assimilated into the displays of contemporary glass. Commissions are awarded by a Museum staff committee. Artists who would like to be considered for selection are encouraged to submit résumés and slides of their work to the Museum.

The Rakow Commission is made possible through the generosity of the late Dr. and Mrs. Leonard S. Rakow, Fellows, friends, and benefactors of the Museum.

Peace, Love, cased, mold-blown, abraded, and enameled. U.S.S.R., Lyubov Ivanovna Savelyeva, the fifth Rakow Commission, 1990. H. (taller) 51.6 cm (90.3.42).

Sculpture from the series "From East to West," blown glass with fused silver leaf and *pâte de verre*, cast bronze fish; copper electroplated, engraved, patinated, and assembled. Japan, Hiroshi Yamano, the sixth Rakow Commission, 1991. H. 74.2 cm (91.6.12).

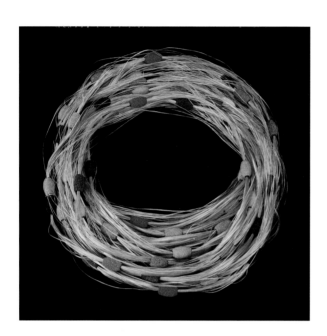

Neckpiece, glass filaments, glass beads, and knotted silk. Austria, Jacqueline Irène Lillie, the seventh Rakow Commission, 1992. D. 28.8 cm (92.3.47).

Commemorative Pokal *Celebrating the 30th Anniversary of the 1962 Toledo Glass Workshops and Fritz Dreisbach's 30 Years of Working with Glass*, blown, applied, cut, and engraved. U.S., Fritz Dreisbach, the eighth Rakow Commission, 1993. H. 54.8 cm (93.4.26).

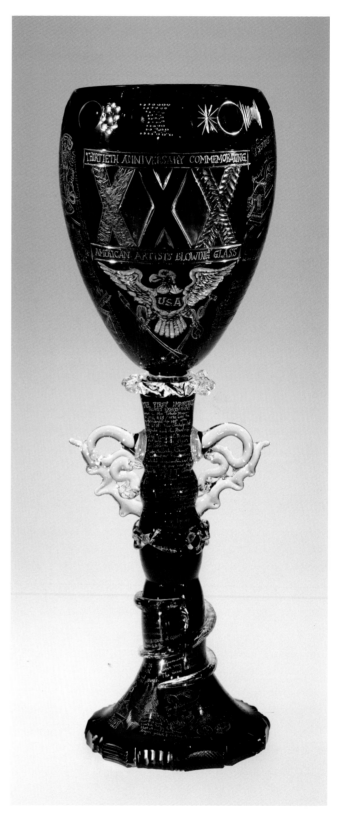

Painting and sculpture, *Mataram*, acid-etched, sandblasted, enameled, and leaded; blown glass boat. Germany, Ursula Huth, the ninth Rakow Commission, 1994. H. 60.0 cm, W. 73.8 cm (94.3.152, 161).

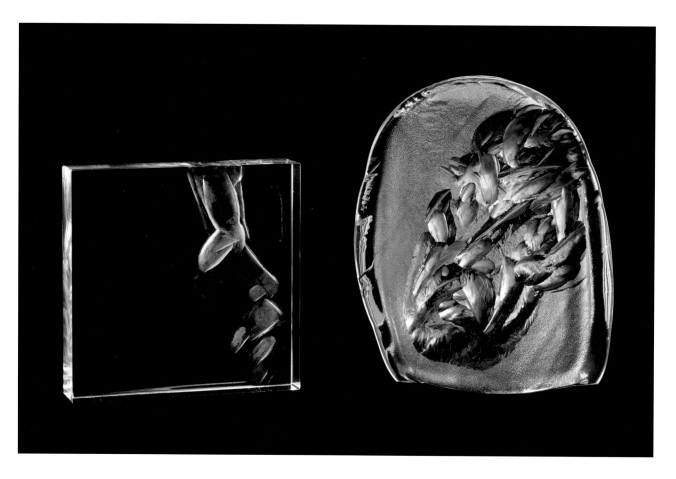

Two Portraits: Václav Havel (LEFT) *and Vladimír Kopecký*, engraved. Czech Republic, Jiří Harcuba, the 10th Rakow Commission, 1995. H. (taller) 27.7 cm (95.3.60, 61).

Hopi, cased and blown, with filigree cane decoration. U.S./Italy, Lino Tagliapietra,
the 11th Rakow Commission, 1996. H. (taller) 69.2 cm (96.4.166).

The Silent, crushed glass melted in a mold and polished; diabase base. Sweden, Ann Wolff, the 12th Rakow Commission, 1997. W. 16.4 cm (97.3.38).

Sculpture, *Bearing*, glass tubes, blown and assembled. U.S., Michael Scheiner, the 13th Rakow Commission, 1998. L. 243.2 cm (98.4.463).

Sculptural vessel, *Niijima*, from "Niijima Vessel Series," fused, hot-formed, and carved. Australia, Klaus Moje, the 14th Rakow Commission, 1999. H. 54.0 cm (99.6.8).

1990–1999
Donors to the Glass Collection

The Museum recognizes with gratitude 701 individuals and institutions whose generosity enriched the collection in the 1990s. The numbers that follow some of the names refer to the numbers of the illustrations that depict their gifts.

Anne and Ronald Abramson, Rockville, Maryland (175)

Maureen and Roger Ackerman, Corning, New York (176)

A/D Gallery, New York, New York

Advanced Refraction Inc., Mountain View, California

William P. Allis, Cambridge, Massachusetts, in memory of Nancy Olive Morison Allis

Al-Majlis International, London, England

Mrs. Eugene E. Anderson Jr., New Canaan, Connecticut, in memory of Mildred Hamilton Locke

Willy Andersson, Kosta, Sweden

Art Alliance for Contemporary Glass, the Creative Glass Center of America, Ben W. Heineman Sr., and Carl H. Pforzheimer III (179)

Martine and Alexandre Asseraf, Corning, New York

Mr. and Mrs. D. Robert Baker, Elmira, New York

Rick Barandes, New York, New York

Marilyn J. Barker, Fort Myers, Florida, in memory of Ora and Julia Byerly

Maeluise Barkin, Rochester, New York

Todd Barlin, Haberfield, Australia

Mr. and Mrs. Richard Barons, Maine, New York

Luis O. Barros, Chicago, Illinois, and Delray Beach, Florida (127)

Arlon Bayliss, Anderson, Indiana

The Beaumont Company, Morgantown, West Virginia

C. Richard Becker, New York, New York

Richard E. Beckwith, Venice, California, in memory of Ernest and Florence Beckwith

Mr. and Mrs. Stephen Beers, North Tarrytown, New York, in memory of Isabel Dorflinger (60)

Allan B. Bell, Seattle, Washington, in memory of Retta A. Bell

Berengo Fine Arts, Murano, Italy

Mr. and Mrs. Edward H. Berg, Newark, Delaware

Julius and Hazel E. Berger, Passaic, New Jersey

Catharine Leffel Birch, Louisville, Kentucky

Frederick Birkhill, Pinckney, Michigan

James H. Black, Mentor, Ohio

Jane Labino Black, Windsor, Ontario, Canada, and Mary Kay Garn, Sylvania, Ohio

Michael Bloch, Copenhagen, Denmark

Harry Blodgett Jr., Corning, New York

Bastiaan Blok, Noordwijk, The Netherlands

Dr. Henry C. Blount Jr., Lexington, Kentucky

Ruth Blumka, New York, New York, in memory of her daughter, Victoria (6)

Andrei Bokotey, Lvov, U.S.S.R.

Milton W. Bond, Stratford, Connecticut

Laurie and Irvin J. Borowsky, Philadelphia, Pennsylvania

Arthur and Mary Boulanger, Ocala, Florida

Boyd Art Glass Collectors Guild, Hatboro, Pennsylvania

Åsa Brandt, Torshalla, Sweden, and Habatat Galleries, Detroit, Michigan

Braunstein/Quay Gallery and Dana Zed, San Francisco, California

Martin Bresler, New York, New York (185)

Harriet Koehler Brett, Elmira Heights, New York

Robert H. Brill, Corning, New York

Lee Broadwin, Morris Plains, New Jersey

David Brokars, by bequest

Mr. and Mrs. James A. Brown, Lancaster, Pennsylvania

Maggie Graham Broyles, Wimberly, Texas

Mrs. Evangeline B. Bruce, Washington, D.C. (122)

Radovan Brychta and Jaroslav Zahradník, Železný Brod, Czech Republic

Mary and Thomas S. Buechner, Corning, New York

Rev. Msgr. Richard K. Burns, by bequest

Edward A. and Louise K. Bush, Corning, New York

Caithness Collectors Society, Garfield, New Jersey

Mr. and Mrs. Matthew Cammen, Painted Post, New York, in memory of Attorney Claude V. Stowell, from his family (102)

Thomas Caple, Hornell, New York

James Carpenter, New York, New York

Mrs. William M. Cassidy Sr., Corning, New York, in memory of William M. Cassidy Sr., from his wife and children

Chatham Glass Co., North Chatham, Massachusetts

Franz Chernak, Lvov, U.S.S.R.

Claude Chesneau, Courville, France

Frank Chiarenza, Newington, Connecticut

Dale Chihuly, Seattle, Washington

Michael E. Clark and Jill Thomas-Clark, Elmira, New York

Mr. and Mrs. Thomas A. Clawson, Buckhannon, West Virginia

Julie Clinton and William C. Stokes, Bellingham, Washington

Barbara Smith Coale, Dearborn, Michigan

Committee for Ernie Davis Celebration, Corning, New York

Norman L. and Patricia Corah, Buffalo and Williamsville, New York

Corning Incorporated, Corning, New York

Corning Incorporated, Wilmington, North Carolina

Vittorio Costantini, Venice, Italy

William R. Coyle, Fort Washington, Maryland

Crystal Art Associates, Ocean, New Jersey

Daniel Swarovski SA, Paris, France

Mr. and Mrs. William E. Davis, Little Rock, Arkansas

James P. Day, Gulfport, Florida, in memory of Mary Joan Day

Bernard Dejonghe, Brianconnet, France

Delomosne & Son Ltd., London, England

Department of Archives and Record Management, Corning Incorporated, Corning, New York

Deutsches Bergbau-Museum, Bochum, Germany

Thomas P. Dimitroff, Corning, New York

Thomas P. Dimitroff, Corning, New York, and Bill Mehlenbach, Cohocton, New York

Mr. and Mrs. Thomas P. Dimitroff, Corning, New York

Thomas P. Dimitroff Family, Corning, New York, in honor of Mr. and Mrs. George J. Burd and Mr. and Mrs. Edgar A. Van Hyning

Polly Dirvin, Ponte Vedra Beach, Florida

DMD Development Manufacturing Distributor, Voorburg, The Netherlands

Albane Dolez, Paris, France

Domus, Milan, Italy

Mr. and Mrs. Jay Doros, Irvington, New Jersey, and Mr. and Mrs. Richard H. Parsons, Morristown, New Jersey

Richard Downes, Larkspur, California

Ruthana Balch Dreisbach, Naples, Florida, in memory of Dale Alson Dreisbach

Alastair Duncan, New York, New York (110)

The Dunlop Collection, Phoenix, Arizona

Evelyn and Mildred Durkin, Corning, New York, in memory of Andrew and Mary Gallagher Durkin

Ecomusée de la Région Fourmies-Trélon, Fourmies, France

Gerald M. Eggert, Rochester, New York

Gift in part of Gerald M. Eggert, Rochester, New York, in memory of Christine Clara Weiss (115)

Gerald M. Eggert, Rochester, New York, in memory of Christine Clara Weiss (116)

G. Eason Eige, Huntington, West Virginia

Erwin Eisch, Frauenau, Germany (165)

Ada E. Ekdahl, Palm Harbor, Florida, in memory of Felix J. Ekdahl (64)

Zakaria Sadek Elkonani, Cairo, Egypt

Gertrude Elliot, Elmira, New York; Mary McDermott and Elizabeth Cheshire, Penn Yan, New York; and Helen Robertson, Wellsboro, Pennsylvania, in memory of George Patrick Nixon and Rachel Hunt Nixon

Elizabeth Elliott, Lilias Outerbridge, Evelina Kats, Harry B. Hollins, Angelica Braestrup, and Brita H. Bonechi, in memory of Elizabeth and Göran Holmquist

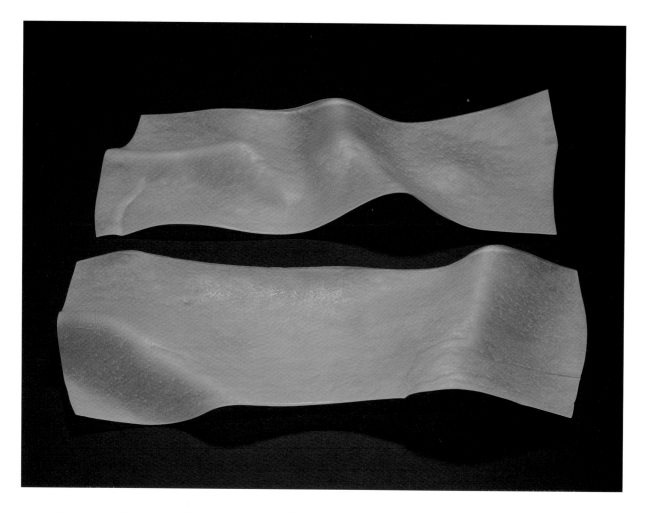

Sculpture, *Parchment*, sheet glass, slumped, cut, and engraved. Germany, Franz Xaver Höller, 1997. L. (larger) 98.0 cm (99.3.98). Photo by Andrew M. Fortune.

Dish on Stone I, II, and *III,* sheet glass, slumped and sandblasted; stone. The Netherlands, Bert Frijns, 1997. D. (largest dish) 51.2 cm (99.3.99–101). Photo by Andrew M. Fortune.

Grace Elliott, Carmel, California, by bequest

Kate Elliott, Seattle, Washington

Gift in part of Elliott-Brown Gallery, Seattle, Washington

Empire State Bottle Collectors Association, New Hartford, New York

Ellen J. Epstein, Mount Kisco, New York

Raymond F. Errett, Corning, New York

Donald and Ursula Farm, Montvale, New Jersey

Stephen Fellerman and Clair Raabe, Sheffield, Massachusetts

T. Reed Ferguson, State College, Pennsylvania

Mr. and Mrs. Joseph Fetcho, Syracuse, New York

Fiam Italia, Tavullia, Italy (139)

Henry Fillebrown, Tivorton, Rhode Island

Jan Fišar, Železný Brod, Czech Republic (155)

Flos Incorporated, Huntington Station, New York

Mrs. Aldus Fogelsanger, Ithaca, New York

Mrs. Lois Sweet Fogelsanger and family, Ithaca, New York

Martin A. Folb, Los Angeles, California, in memory of his parents, Alex and Ruth Folb

Marilyn Q. Fomon, New York, New York

Robert Quaintance Fomon, New York, New York, in memory of William C. Anderson, president and manager of the American Cut Glass Company, Lansing, Michigan (103)

Raymond and Marie Fontaine, Fort Lauderdale, Florida

Mrs. John E. Ford, Wooster, Ohio, in memory of Helen Hoover Secrest

Forma and Design, Norwalk, Connecticut

Dr. Lawrence Fornald, Lake Ariel, Pennsylvania

Fostoria Ohio Glass Association, Fostoria, Ohio

John P. Fox Jr., Corning, New York

Susanne K. Frantz, Corning, New York, and Paradise Valley, Arizona

Mrs. Ruth-Maria Franz, Vienna, Austria

Elsa Freund, Eureka Springs, Arkansas

James Friant, Ocean City, New Jersey

Barry Friedman, New York, New York

Irene A. Friedman and family, Union, New Jersey

Lt. Col. Dean R. Frohnapple, Slanesville, West Virginia

Linda and Kirk Fugle, South Livonia, New York

William Furth, New York, New York

Mr. and Mrs. Lee Gainsborough, Philadelphia, Pennsylvania

Mary Adria Galbraith, Clifton Park, New York, in memory of her parents, Mary Grant Galbraith and Den J. Galbraith

Lorraine Galinsky, Cold Spring Harbor, New York

Saara Gallin, White Plains, New York

Paul V. Gardner, by bequest (130)

Angeline Gaultieri, Erie, Pennsylvania

Mrs. Ruth L. Gay, Midland, Ontario, Canada (granddaughter of Walter Egginton) (96–98)

Alison Cornwall Geissler, Edinburgh, Scotland

Family of Bruce R. Gibbs, in his memory (95)

Glasexport Company Ltd., Liberec, Czech Republic

Javier Gómez, Madrid, Spain

Don S. Gong and family, Rochester, New York, in memory of Sue Ha Tang

Gary Goodrich, Frankfort, Kentucky

John C. Goodrich, Truro, Massachusetts, in memory of Elsie Moore Price

Dr. and Mrs. Abbot Lee Granoff, Norfolk, Virginia, from the estate of their uncle, Sam Weisbord

Susan Kemp Gray, Wilmington, Delaware

Daniel Greenberg and Susan Steinhauser, Los Angeles, California

Purchased with the assistance of Daniel Greenberg and Susan Steinhauser, Los Angeles, California (171)

Daniel Greenberg and Susan Steinhauser, Los Angeles, California, with the assistance of Ruth T. Summers and Richard Marquis

Arthur and Theresa Greenblatt, Lambertville, New Jersey (117)

Ronald James Griswold, Arlington, Virginia, in memory of Mr. and Mrs. James Semple and Marilyn Semple Liese

Kurt Groeger, Corning, New York

Herbert C. Gross Jr., Media, Pennsylvania

Lee and Ray Grover, Naples, Florida, in honor of Ruth Suppes

Leonore K. Grover, Naples, Florida

William Gudenrath, New York and Corning, New York

Arthur W. Guenther, Millington, New Jersey, in memory of Imogen Ireson Guenther

Donald L. Guile, Horseheads, New York

Barbara Habig, Jasper, Tennessee

Dorothy Hafner, New York, New York (186)

David G. Hale and Margaret Lenderking Hale, Brockport, New York, in memory of Edna Bickett Lenderking and in honor of Howard Lenderking

Mr. and Mrs. Donald S. Hall, Rochester, New York

Horace N. Hall, Collegeville, Pennsylvania, in memory of Dionysius Nill

Eiko Hamada, Jamesville, New York, in memory of Kotaro Hamada

The Hamblen Trust of the Hamblen Family: Watt and Tallie Hamblen, Mary Margaret and Mattie Terry Hamblen (81, 83)

Harmer Rooke Galleries, New York, New York

Mrs. Penrose Hawkes, Corning, New York, in memory of Penrose Hawkes

Ben W. Heineman Family, Chicago, Illinois (161, 162)

Douglas and Michael Heller, New York, New York

Heller Gallery and an anonymous donor, New York, New York

Her Majesty Queen Margrethe of Denmark and His Royal Highness the Prince Consort, Copenhagen, Denmark

Mrs. Alberta Herman, Peoria, Illinois

Jane Hershey, Sarasota, Florida (172)

Helen Carew Hickman, Lancaster, Pennsylvania

Michael Higgins, Riverside, Illinois

Rose Mary Highman, Boulder, Colorado

Kimiake and Shinichi Higuchi, Saitama, Japan

Beth Hin, Rochester, New York, in honor of Mr. and Mrs. William G. Hin, from their children

Historical Society of Western Pennsylvania, Pittsburgh, Pennsylvania

Janet B. Hoffman, Painted Post, New York

Janet B. Hoffman, Painted Post, New York, and Southampton, Pennsylvania, in memory of Dr. Parker Hoffman

Winifred M. Holaday, by bequest

Mrs. Raymond G. Horner, Englewood, Colorado

Harry Horvitz, Evanston, Illinois

Hon. and Mrs. Amory Houghton, Corning, New York (28)

Amory Houghton Jr., Corning, New York

Mr. and Mrs. James R. Houghton, Corning, New York (178)

Maisie Houghton, Corning, New York; Sylvia Baldwin, Rhinecliff, New York; and Elizabeth Kinnicutt, Lincolnville, Maine, in memory of their mother, Sybil Jay Waldron

Houghton Endowment (27)

Purchased with the assistance of Houghton Endowment (104)

John and Catherine Hoxie, Corning, New York

Fred Hoyt, Rolling Meadows, Illinois

Hulet Glass, McKinleyville, California

Ursula Huth, Weil im Schönbuch, Germany

Clyde E. Ingersoll, Tonawanda, New York

Mrs. George Ingham, Naples, Florida, in memory of her husband (32)

Iwata Glass Company, Tokyo, Japan

Mr. and Mrs. Meyer Jacobson, Houston, Texas

Jacques Jugeat Inc., New York, New York

Isabel V. James, East Aurora, New York, and Susan V. Shields, Indianapolis, Indiana, in memory of their grandmother, Isabel Stilwell Vaughan

Weston H. Jenkins, Corning, New York

Mrs. Shirley Jennings, Albuquerque, New Mexico

Larry Jessen, Frederick, Maryland

Roland E. Jester, St. Louis, Missouri

Jody & Darrell's Glass Collectibles, Arlington, Texas

Edward G. (Ted) Jolda, Parksville, British Columbia, Canada

Edith A. Jones, Bethesda, Maryland

Grace Jones, Burnt Hills, New York, in memory of Jackson and Grace Walton Blank

Cliff and Ruth Jordan, Meridale, New York (84)

Caroline L. Jossem, Churchville, New York, in memory of Bert H. Jossem

Robert M. and Nedra Joyce, Sun City Center, Florida

Joan and Robert Judelson, Park City, Utah

Rossella Junck, Venice, Italy

Dr. Peter Kaellgren, Toronto, Ontario, Canada

Sanford Kalb, Howell, New Jersey

Mr. and Mrs. Leo Kaplan, New York, New York

Mr. and Mrs. Leo Kaplan, New York, New York, in honor of Emanuel Lacher

Leo, Ruth, and Alan Kaplan, and Susan Kaplan Jacobson, New York, New York

Erica Karawina, Honolulu, Hawaii

Karuna Glass, Lowell, Ohio

Carol and John Kelly, Towson, Maryland

John Eliot Kennedy, Grasonville, Maryland

Balloon-I, blown and cut. Germany, Franz Xaver Höller, 1994. D. 44.0 cm (99.3.97). Photo by Andrew M. Fortune.

Mabel and Calvin McCamy, Wappingers Falls, New York

Omega Woodall McCord, Winchester, Tennessee

Michael McDonough, New York, New York

Dan R. McFarland, Dublin, Ohio

Mary Allyene (Roland) McKinley, Prescott, Arizona

Martha Warren McKinney, Big Flats, New York

Leila L. McKnight, Washington, D.C. (74)

Laura McMahon, Horseheads, New York

Edward R. Meddaugh, Elmira, New York

Marcel Mégroz, Schottikou, Switzerland, and René Mégroz, Winterthur, Switzerland

Elsie Melby, Duluth, Minnesota

Jim Melka, Villa Park, Illinois

Mr. and Mrs. Peter Meltzer, New York, New York

Gertrude Christman Melvin Endowment (65)

Deborah Menkers, New Windsor, New York, in memory of Yette London

Jean and Martin Mensch, New York, New York

M. Sean Mercer, Harrisonburg, Virginia

Ursula Merker, Kelheim, Germany

Meyerson & Nowinski Art Associates and Ginny Ruffner, Seattle, Washington

Lynn Mickals, Watkins Glen, New York

Tom Mignalt, Flagstaff, Arizona

Riko Mikami, Nagano-ken, Japan

Jim W. Miller, Harrison, Arkansas, in honor of his parents, Joe and Francis Miller (89)

William S. and Helen M. Miller, Sebring, Florida

Miller Gallery, New York, New York

James Minson, Seattle, Washington

Natsue Mohri, Tokyo, Japan

Mansour Mokhtarzadeh, London, England

Carmine Monteforte and Virginia Stone, Amityville, New York

Phyllis Montgomery, Santa Fe, New Mexico

Carlo Moretti, Murano, Italy

Giusy Moretti, Venice, Italy

F. Brockett Morey, Painted Post, New York

Ann Morhauser, Santa Cruz, California

Isobel Lee Moulton, Hightstown, New Jersey

Keiko Mukaide, Kanagawa, Japan

Kathleen Mulcahy, Oakdale, Pennsylvania

Betty Murray, Princeton, New Jersey

Brian Musselwhite and Conrad Biernacki, Toronto, Ontario, Canada

Suzanne Nady, by bequest

Robert Naess, Cavendish, Vermont

Purchased with the assistance of Mr. and Mrs. Paul Nassau, New York, New York

Mr. and Mrs. M. R. Nathan, London, England

National Heisey Glass Museum, Newark, Ohio

Raphael Nemeth, New York, New York

Albert Nesle, New York, New York

The New Bedford Glass Society, New Bedford, Massachusetts

Charles G. Nitsche, Geneseo, New York, in memory of Clement F. J. Nitsche

Joseph V. Noble, Maplewood, New Jersey

Window, cut and leaded glass. U.S., designed by Adler and Sullivan for the Auditorium and Tower Building, Chicago, Illinois, 1886–1889. H. (frame) 87.3 cm (93.4.16). Clara S. Peck Endowment.

Nordic Art Glass, Colorado Springs, Colorado

Mrs. R. Henry Norweb Jr., Willoughby, Ohio, in memory of the Hon. R. Henry Norweb (31)

John Nygren, Walnut Cove, North Carolina, in memory of Carl G. Nygren

Mrs. Isabel Obourn, Painted Post, New York, in memory of Boleslaw Bonicave

Richard O'Brien, Corning, New York

Mr. and Mrs. Richard A. O'Brien, Corning, New York

Cornelius O'Donnell Jr., Corning, New York

Kevin O'Grady, Santa Fe, New Mexico

Mary Ellen Olcott, Myrtle Beach, South Carolina

Mrs. Arline B. Oliphant, Tulsa, Oklahoma, in the name of Narsha Butler

Mr. and Mrs. John K. Olsen, St. Petersburg, Florida

Gift in part of Dennis Oppenheim, New York, New York

Mrs. Elizabeth Oppenheim, Berkeley, California

Orrefors AB, Orrefors, Sweden

Debra A. Ortello, Cheshire, Connecticut, in memory of her husband, Vincent Ortello

Daniel Ostroff, Los Angeles, California

Dr. Jutta-Annette and Philip S. Page, Montour Falls, New York

Painted Soda Bottle Collectors Association, La Mesa, California

Mr. and Mrs. Richard H. Parsons, Morristown, New Jersey

Mrs. Esther Kretschmann Patch, Corning, New York

Maurice and Harriet Paul, Rice Lake, Wisconsin

Molly Pearse and Barbara James, Chipley, Florida, in memory of Madeline Martin Purdy and S. Ames Purdy

Clara S. Peck Endowment (pages 8 and 122; 106, 107)

Purchased with the assistance of Clara S. Peck Endowment (3)

Sylva Petrová, Prague, Czechoslovakia

Carl H. and Betty Pforzheimer, Scarsdale, New York

Mr. and Mrs. Carlton Phillips, Painted Post, New York

Thurman Pierce, New York, New York

Robert F. Pigeon, Mesa, Arizona, in memory of Francis and Ilse Pigeon

Pilchuck Glass School, Seattle, Washington

The Pilgrim Glass Corporation, Ceredo, West Virginia

Jean Pire, Engis, Belgium

Dorothy and Charles J. Plohn Jr., Princeton, New Jersey (18)

Walter Poeth, Oakland, California (77, 82)

PPG Industries Inc., Pittsburgh, Pennsylvania

Priscilla B. Price, Nelson, Pennsylvania

Mr. and Mrs. Charles Puckette, Scotia, New York

Wilmot L. Putnam Jr., Corning, New York; Raymond and Judith Putnam, Corning, New York; Michele Putnam, Horseheads, New York; and Jeb and Louise Putnam, Richmond, Virginia

James Quiring, Cape Coral, Florida, and Allan Quiring, Greer, South Carolina

Sally and Michael Rabkin, Los Angeles, California

Mrs. Leonard S. Rakow, Bronx, New York (46)

Mrs. Leonard S. Rakow, by bequest (48, 49)

Bruce and Adele Randall, Syosset, New York (113)

Peter Rath, Vienna, Austria

Mrs. Joseph Rauh, Washington, D.C.

Robert and Elizabeth Raymond, Lawrence, Kansas, in memory of Ida Gleason Raymond

Joan E. Raz, Tigard, Oregon

Mr. and Mrs. Richard C. Reedy, Wakefield, Massachusetts

Gladys W. Richards and Paul C. Richards, Middletown, Rhode Island (52)

Prof. Dr. Claus Josef Riedel, Schneegattern, Austria

Mrs. E. P. Rittershausen, South Burlington, Vermont

Ritzenhoff Cristal, Marsberg, Germany

Mr. and Mrs. Lawrence S. Rivkin, Show Low, Arizona

Theodore D. Robinson II, Villanova, Pennsylvania

Robert Rockwell III, Corning, New York

Rockwell Museum and Robert Rockwell III, Corning, New York

Clara Steacy Rogers and George L. Rogers, Ava, New York, in memory of John R. and Elizabeth M. Steacy

Richard and Ann Rohrberg, Rochester, New York

Mary M. Rollins, Houston, Texas

Stewart Rosenblum, New York, New York

Rosenthal Aktiengellschaft Design Studio, Bayern, Federal Republic of Germany

Mr. and Mrs. Ned Rubin, Penn Yan, New York, in memory of Etta Rubin

Mr. and Mrs. Stephen K. Ruoff, Rochester, New York, in memory of James S. and Mary K. Ruoff

Mr. and Mrs. Howard E. Russell, New Castle, New Hampshire

Sara Stedman Russell, McLean, Virginia, in memory of Isabel Leighton Hall (59)

Sara Stedman Russell, McLean, Virginia, in memory of Barbara Hall Stedman

Jaromír Rybák, Prague, Czech Republic

Mr. and Mrs. Frieder Ryser, Bern, Switzerland

Louis O. St. Aubin Jr., New Bedford, Massachusetts

Mr. and Mrs. Albert E. St. Denis, Syracuse, New York

Seymour Salem, Mamaroneck, New York

Gladys F. Salisbury, Punta Gorda, Florida, and Richard B. Rothrock and Crystal B. Janaskie, Port Charlotte, Florida, in memory of Shelby Rothrock

Donald Samick, Ghent, New York

Laura de Santillana, Venice, Italy

Giovanni Sarpellon, Venice, Italy

Jaci Saunders and family, Corning, New York

Mr. and Mrs. George B. Saxe, Palo Alto, California

Albin Schaedel, Arnstadt, Germany

Mr. and Mrs. Richard Schenk, Heber Springs, Arkansas

Richard Lee Schiffman, by bequest

Clementine Mills Schlaikjer and Jes Erich Schlaikjer, by bequest (75)

Peter Schreiber & Co., Gossau, Switzerland

Samuel Schwartz, Clifton, New Jersey

Samuel Schwartz, Clifton, New Jersey, in memory of Esther Ipp Schwartz (61)

Arlene Palmer Schwind, Yarmouth, Maine

George Scott, Edinburgh, Scotland

Pair of covered tankards, blown; copper-gilt mounts. Europe, probably Bohemia, possibly France, second half of 19th century. OH. 22.0 cm (91.3.69). Gift of Mrs. J. McCullough Turner.

Frederick S. Seib, Lake San Marcos, California, in memory of Mr. and Mrs. Frederick G. Seib

L. H. Selman, Santa Cruz, California

Art Seymour, Doyle, California

Marvin S. Shadel, Alexandria, Virginia, in memory of Elizabeth Shadel (100)

John and Laura Shelton, Williamsburg, Virginia

Christopher Sheppard, London, England

Benedict Silverman, New York, New York (112)

Gift in part of Benedict Silverman, New York, New York, in memory of Gerry Lou Silverman (105)

Malvina and Stanley Silverman, Ventnor, New Jersey, in memory of Bessie Silverman

Josh Simpson, Shelburne Falls, Massachusetts

Estelle F. Sinclaire, Jamesburg, New Jersey

Estelle F. Sinclaire, Jamesburg, New Jersey, in memory of Thurman R. Pierce Jr., and in memory of Carolyn Sinclaire Van Mater, from her family

Anna Skibska, Poland

Skrufs Glasbruk AB, Skruv, Sweden

Nikita Borisovich Smirnov, St. Petersburg, U.S.S.R.

Harriet Smith, Roxbury, New York (63, 78, 86, 92)

James O. Smith, Lawrence, Kansas

Robert V. Smith, Downingtown, Pennsylvania

Gladys M. and Harry A. Snyder Memorial Trust (54, 62, 79)

Purchased with the assistance of Gladys M. and Harry A. Snyder Memorial Trust (91)

Torben Sode, Copenhagen and Vanlose, Denmark

Ann Southworth, Somers, New York

Judi Jordan Sowers, Brooklyn, New York (141)

Robert Sowers, by bequest and in memory of Theresa Obermayr Sowers (142)

Betty Gruene Speir, Valley Falls, New York

Jane Shadel Spillman, Corning, New York

Patricia A. Stankard, Mantua, New Jersey

Mr. and Mrs. Paul J. Stankard, Mantua, New Jersey

Starlight, Dobbs Ferry, New York

Frank Starr, Corning, New York

Frank Starr, Corning, New York, in memory of Robert B. Starr

Dorothy Hall Staubus, York, Pennsylvania, by bequest

Mr. and Mrs. Howard Stein, New York, New York (114)

The Steinberg Foundation, Vaduz, Liechtenstein (148–154)

Steuben, Corning, New York

Steuben, Design Department, New York, New York

Steuben and Joel A. Smith, Corning, New York (184)

Bonnie Stillman, Cameron Mills, New York

Paul Stillman, Cameron Mills, New York

Mr. and Mrs. Paul Stillman, Cameron Mills, New York

The Stillman Family, Cameron Mills, New York

Ellen and Gilbert S. Stoewsand, Geneva, New York

Mrs. Rudolf von Strasser, Vienna, Austria

Mrs. Jerome Strauss, State College, Pennsylvania

Dorothy Mae Strouse, by bequest

Loren Stump, Elk Grove, California

Mrs. Raymond Suppes, Chevy Chase, Maryland

Frank O. Swanson, Livonia, Michigan

Swarovski America Ltd., Cranston, Rhode Island

Swarovski Collectors Society, Cranston, Rhode Island

Elizabeth Swenson, Ocean City, New Jersey, in memory of Arne Swenson

Lino Tagliapietra, Seattle, Washington

Lino Tagliapietra, Seattle, Washington, and Susanne K. Frantz, Corning, New York

Tehas Tarbeklass, Tallinn, Estonia

Dr. and Mrs. Julius Tarshis, Scarsdale, New York

Lauren Tarshis, New York, New York

Kay and Del Tarsitano, Valley Stream, New York

Charles Taylor, Newport, Rhode Island, in memory of Edla Guihild Taylor

Dr. Wayne C. Templer, Corning, New York, in memory of Dr. and Mrs. Willis C. Templer

Jill Thomas-Clark, Elmira, New York

Raymond and Virginia Thompson, Lake Bay, Washington

Mrs. Sarah Hawkes Thornton, Rochester, New York

Catherine Thuro, Toronto, Ontario, Canada

Tiffin Glass Collectors Club, Tiffin, Ohio

Emmanuel Tiliakos, Winchester, Massachusetts

The Toledo Museum of Art, Toledo, Ohio, for study

Sam Tolkin, Santa Monica, California

Margit Toth, Csobánka, Hungary

Milon Townsend, Hilton, New York

Erik Tozzi, New York, New York

Victor Trabucco, Clarence, New York

Adolph A. Trinidad Jr., Pearl River, New York

Mr. and Mrs. Glenn W. Tripp, Los Angeles, California

Mr. and Mrs. Thomas R. Trowbridge III, New York, New York

Mrs. J. McCullough Turner, Bethany, Connecticut (page 124)

Margaret Van Etten, Jamestown, New York

Annalien van Kempen, Voorburg, The Netherlands

Mr. and Mrs. Philip Van Mater, Marlboro, New York, in memory of Carolyn Sinclaire Van Mater, from her family

John W. Van Zanten, Corning, New York

Mrs. Florence Emilson Vang, Corning, New York, in memory of Hugo and Genevieve Walter Emilson, and in memory of William Vang and his parents, Eugene and Agda Vang

Dita Varleta, North Haven, Connecticut

Mrs. William J. Vay, San Diego, California

Venini S.p.A., Venice, Italy

M. Vest and T. Sode, Vanløse, Denmark

Virginia Museum of Fine Arts, Richmond, Virginia

Kurt Wallstab, Dürrenkopf, Federal Republic of Germany

The Waterford Society, Wall, New Jersey

Mrs. David G. Watterson, Cleveland, Ohio

Dorothy White Wehrstedt, Pittsburgh, Pennsylvania, in memory of Norbert T. White (87)

Gladys D. Weinberg, Columbia, Missouri

David J. Weinstein, New York, New York

David J. Weiss, Los Angeles, California

Citrus fruit, blown and applied. Italy, Venice, about 1700. H. (tallest) 17.0 cm (99.3.34–36). Gift of Rainer Zietz.

David B. Whitehouse, Corning, New York

Charles P. Whittemore, Kent, Connecticut (70)

Francis Whittemore, Lansdale, Pennsylvania

Camilla M. Wiener and Frank F. Wiener, Narragansett, Rhode Island, in honor of Dr. William A. Turnbaugh and Sarah Peabody Turnbaugh

Donald and Carol Wiiken, Oak Park, Illinois

E. Crosby Willet, Philadelphia, Pennsylvania

Harold S. Williams, Monroeton, Pennsylvania

Harold S. Williams, Monroeton, Pennsylvania, in memory of "Hettie" Williams

Mr. and Mrs. Nicholas Williams, Corning, New York

Kenneth M. Wilson, Punta Gorda, Florida

Elizabeth Wistar, by bequest

Roland Wolcott, Corning, New York

Lyuba and Ernesto Wolf, Paris, France (4)

Mrs. Alfred Wolkenberg, New York, New York

Walter Woodcock, Corning, New York, in memory of Caroline J. Woodcock, from her family

D. Stratton Woodruff, Bryn Mawr, Pennsylvania

The Worshipful Company of Glass Sellers of London, London, England

Jerry E. Wright, Corning, New York (129)

Virginia Wright, Corning, New York

The Wunsch Americana Foundation, New York, New York

The Wunsch Foundation Inc., New York, New York

F. Yazdani, London, England

Yokohama Museum of Art, Yokohama, Japan

Christine York, Bellaire, Texas

Mrs. Helen York, Houston, Texas

Patricia J. Younie, Seattle, Washington

Alan Youse, Port Townsend, Washington

Rainer Zietz, London, England (page 125)

Mr. and Mrs. Martin Zigovsky, Newland, North Carolina, in memory of Katherine Zigovsky

Jörg F. Zimmermann, Uhingen, Federal Republic of Germany

Index of Artists, Designers, and Factories

Plaque with female figure, *pâte de verre*. France, Henry Cros, about 1886. H. 13.5 cm (96.3.23).